REIMAGINE

Preaching in the
Present Tense

**Mark Whittall's reflections are fresh, honest, gracious and
inspiring.** He openly shares his struggle to engage with the
Sunday lectionary in the context of his daily life as a Chris-
tian pilgrim and as a preacher and leader of a congregation.
This will be a useful resource for any follower of Jesus
who is interested in another disciple's journey and ministry.
I found it refreshed and challenged me.
– The Right Rev. Mary Irwin-Gibson, Bishop, Diocese of
Montreal, Anglican Church of Canada

I would love a double portion of Mark Whittall's courage.
Where most of us shy away, Mark clears his voice, and speaks
a word from the Lord. No wonder his parish in Ottawa is
flourishing. This is a model for preaching in mainline liberal
parishes across Canada and beyond.
– Jason Byassee, Butler Chair in Homiletics and Biblical
Hermeneutics at the Vancouver School of Theology

**These thoughtful and engaging homilies take questions
raised by everyday events and put them in conversation
with the readings of the day.** I love the introductions that
show how important it is to wrestle with both event and
scripture in preparing to preach.
– Patricia Bays, author of *This Anglican Church of Ours*

Mark Whittall

ReImagine

Preaching in the
Present Tense

WOOD LAKE

Editor: Mike Schwartzentruber
Designer: Robert MacDonald
Proofreader: Dianne Greenslade

Library and Archives Canada Cataloguing in Publication
Whittall, Mark, 1962-, author
ReImagine : preaching in the present tense / Mark Whittall.
Includes bibliographical references.
Issued also in print and electronic formats.
ISBN 978-1-77064-921-7 (softcover).—ISBN 978-1-77064-922-4 (HTML)
1. Topical preaching. 2. Preaching. I. Title.
BV4235.T65W45 2017 251 C2017-905840-1 C2017-905841-X

ISBN 978-1-77064-921-7

Published by Wood Lake Publishing Inc.
485 Beaver Lake Road, Kelowna, BC, Canada, V4V 1S5
www.woodlake.com I 250.766.2778

We acknowledge the financial support of the Government of Canada. Nous
reconnaissons l'appui financier du gouvernement du Canada. Wood Lake
Publishing acknowledges the financial support of the Province of British
Columbia through the Book Publishing Tax Credit.

At Wood Lake Publishing, we practice what we publish, being guided by a
concern for fairness, justice, and equal opportunity in all of our
relationships with employees and customers. Wood Lake Publishing is
committed to caring for the environment and all creation. Wood Lake
Publishing recycles and reuses, and encourages readers to do the same.
Books are printed on 100% post-consumer recycled paper, whenever
possible. A percentage of all profit is donated to charitable organizations.

Printed in Canada. Printing 10 9 8 7 6 5 4 3 2 1

TABLE OF CONTENTS

Introduction: Preaching in the Present Tense 9

ONE: Power in a Name 15

TWO: Witness among the Stones 23

THREE: I Will Not Keep Silent 29

FOUR: Where You Put Your Body.............................. 37

FIVE: Surely We're Not Blind, Are We? 45

SIX: Evolution 57

SEVEN: Why Bad Things Happen 67

EIGHT: A Brutal Year 75

NINE: Glory 83

TEN: How Dare We?... 91

ELEVEN: Doubt, Singularities, and the Big Bang 99

TWELVE: Dagobah, Emmaus, and the Recognition Problem ...107

THIRTEEN: The First Stone... 115

FORRTEEN: Something More 125

FIFTEEN: It's Time.. 133

SIXTEEN: The Better Story 149

DEDICATION

To my parents, Carole and Phil.

ACKNOWLEDGMENTS

What has been is what will be,
and what has been done is what will be done;
there is nothing new under the sun.
Is there a thing of which it is said,
"See, this is new"?
It has already been,
in the ages before us.
– Ecclesiastes 1:9–10 *(NRSV)*

Perhaps the author of Ecclesiastes had preaching in mind when he set down these words. A preacher is always on the lookout for ideas and stories that can be shaped into the next sermon. I know that my practice is to collect thoughts and images from commentaries and conversations. These then make their way into the sermon, sometimes knowingly, sometimes not, more often than not unacknowledged. So under the heading of acknowledgements, let me try to rectify at least some of these omissions.

I am indebted to those who have taught me homiletics: Kevin Flynn, Anna Carter Florence, Ruthanna Hooke, Gary Hauch, and Thomas Long among others. I owe much to the preachers who have been my colleagues in seminars and workshops, who have shared their ideas with me and provided feedback on my sermons. I am equally indebted to those whose writings, commentaries, and blogs I turn to again and again: Barbara Brown Taylor, David Lose, and the many contributors to the Working Preacher website. All of you will find your ideas and influence scattered throughout this book.

Stories are told and sermons are preached in community. The communities that have shared their stories with me and that have shaped the sermons in this book with their listening and encouragement are St. Albans Church in Ottawa, the parish of Huntley in Carp, and the Church of the Ascension in Ottawa. I am honoured by those who have trusted me with their stories.

I am grateful to my friends and colleagues who have read all or part of this book and who provided me with encouragement and helpful comments along the way: John Wright, Michelle Whittall, Jennifer McCrea-Logie, Tony Whittall, Peter Crosby, Clair Ingles, and Rob Crosby-Shearer. Thanks to my early morning friends at Writeshop Wednesdays in Ottawa – Allison, Lee, John, Kaite, and the rest – where some of these chapters got their start. Thank you to my editor Mike Schwartzentruber and to the team at Wood Lake Publishing; I enjoy working with you.

Most importantly, I would like to thank my family: Guylaine, Jonathan, and Michelle for their love and support, not to mention their advice, comments, and encouragement along the way. This book is dedicated to my parents, Carole and Phil, who have always been there for me. Thanks.

INTRODUCTION

Preaching in the Present Tense

Last night there was a shooting. A masked gunman entered a mosque and opened fire killing six people at evening prayer. The attack wasn't in my hometown, but it wasn't far away. It was in a place I know well, where friends and family live. There is a feeling of helplessness that comes with such news. I turn on the television. I scan the newspapers. I pray. I go to a vigil. These responses I hold in common with others. But then I open the Bible and turn to the scripture readings that will be read on Sunday. For I am a preacher, and on Sunday the people with whom I gather to worship will be asking the question, "What does this mean?"

The sermon is the one place in our worship where people have every right to expect engagement with the question, "What does this mean?" In churches with a tradition of biblical preaching, the word "this" in that question refers, in the first instance, to the biblical texts that are proclaimed. As preachers, our task is to open up the scriptures and to reflect on them, to tell people what we have seen and heard in the text and to say what we believe about it.[1] But the question of meaning goes beyond the world of the biblical text. People want to know what this means for them, for us, today, in the context of all that is going on in our lives and the world around us.

Preaching, in other words, must operate in the present tense. If preaching is to matter, it must speak in and of the present. Thomas

Long, in his book *Preaching from Memory to Hope*, laments the "curious loss of the present tense in much contemporary preaching." Then he puts his finger on what he believes is the problem: "the reluctance of preachers to name the presence and activity of God in our midst."[2]

This reluctance has a history. In premodern times, it was much easier to name the presence and activity of God in our midst. The presence of God in the experience of someone dwelling in Europe in the year 1500 was practically undeniable.[3] The cosmic order testified to divine purpose and action, and the great events of the natural world – floods, earthquakes, and the like – were understood to be acts of God. The social structures of both kingdom and church were grounded in divine authority and interwoven with religious ritual. Our ancestors lived in what has been called an "enchanted" world, a cosmos of meaning and spirits, of demons and moral forces that impinged on human life. In such a world, in such a "social imaginary" to use the language of the philosopher Charles Taylor, it was almost impossible not to feel God's presence.

The disappearance of these modes of God's felt-presence in much of the world over the last 500 years has allowed for what sociologist Max Weber called "disenchantment." Disenchantment is the modern condition that favours reliance on scientific investigation and a rational understanding of events. The result is that the context for belief has changed in our secular age. Some people have simply ceased believing in the divine. Even for those who continue to believe, God may seem distant. For deists, God is remote and no longer involved in the affairs of the world. For interventionists, God is equally remote but will intervene from time to time as needed. But neither a deist nor an interventionist view does justice to the biblical understanding of a God who is intimately involved in our lives, in history, and in creation. Both the deist and interventionist perspectives would corroborate a diminished sense of God in the world rather than seek to restore our awareness of the divine.

An alternative is to develop anew our perception of God's

presence, not by retreating and trying to restore modes of social imagination that existed 500 years ago, but by becoming attuned once more to the divine in-dwelling in our midst.

One example is the "ordinary mysticism" suggested by the theologian Karl Rahner, who predicted in the 1970s that "the devout Christian of the future will either be a 'mystic,' one who has experienced 'something,' or he will cease to be anything at all."[4] To be human, according to Rahner, is to be open to the possibility of God's self-communication. God is experienced in ordinary life.

The preacher's task, then, is to articulate this experience, to name the presence and activity of God in our midst, and in so doing become something of a midwife for ordinary mystics. That's a tall order and there are many paths a preacher can take. The path advocated in this book is one that seeks to connect the biblical stories we encounter in worship with stories that are drawn from the life of the community. The events, encounters, and experiences that form the ordinary and extraordinary narratives of our personal and communal existence, and of our society and culture more broadly, are put into conversation with the scripture readings proclaimed each Sunday. Preaching becomes an opportunity to draw meaning out of these shared stories by naming the presence and action of God in our midst.

When we put our stories into conversation with the biblical text, two things can emerge. The first is that the biblical text is brought to life, allowing the text to engage us and helping us to perceive its relevance. The second is that the biblical text helps us to interpret our own stories, drawing out the meaning we seek, providing us with language, and offering us patterns and scripts that help us to see and name the divine in our midst.[5]

To preach out of the stuff of our lives is to speak in the wisdom tradition. By that I don't mean a form of preaching that doles out practical wisdom and advice for leading a better life. I mean a way of speaking that relies on the conviction that God is present and active in our lives, here and now, in our time and place. I mean that God breaks into human lives to give us an experience of the divine, that we can encounter God in ordinary things, that we can find meaning in everyday life. This wisdom tradition has its roots in scripture, in books like Job and Proverbs, and in the teachings of Jesus.

Biblical preaching in the wisdom tradition is a way of articulating our experience of the divine by putting our stories into conversation with the stories of the Bible, those same sacred texts that our ancestors have been using to articulate holy meaning for thousands of years. To preach biblically requires us to enter the text, to stand in the text, to wrestle with it, to listen in silence, to pray it, to poke it and prod it, to let it poke and prod us, until something happens, until something resonates, until we see something that is true, something true and of God. But in the particular moment that we enter a text, the articulation that rings true for us will be shaped by where we stand. For we stand not only in the text, but also in the midst of our own life story. We live in the currents and countercurrents of people, places and events that flow all around us and that sometimes threaten to knock us off our feet. How the text reveals its truth will be shaped by where we stand on any given day.

The preacher's task is to see and speak that truth and in so doing to bridge the gap between the story of the ancient text and the story we live in now. The "memories, conversations, experiences and hopes" that the community share become the fabric from which the sermon is made.[6] But the preacher must also tell the truth – the truth about what happens when a biblical text intersects the events of our lives and lays claim on us.[7]

We live in a universe of meaning. We experience meaning through history and in community. We were made to make meaning. That's who we are. Rarely are we content to simply catalogue the stuff of our lives as a series of random occurrences. We interpret data as events. We turn events into stories. We tell, and retell our stories in order to discover, generate, and share the meaning which we crave, the meaning that makes our lives intelligible, purposeful, and of value. "When all is said and done," Barbara Brown Taylor observes, "faith may be nothing more than the assignment of holy meaning to events that others call random."[8]

Short, powerful talks that take the stuff of life and convey it as a narrative of meaning and purpose have never been so popular. The global TED Talk phenomenon is a case in point. So too are the slam poets. Preaching has much in common with these meaning-making activities. But there is more.

I preach because I believe that the word of God is a living, dynamic force with the power to change lives. Whenever the word is preached, there exists the potential for a life-changing encounter with God, for the preacher and for the people who have gathered. The stakes are high. The meaning we seek in preaching is not mere human invention nor social convention. Our goal is not so much to make meaning as to tap into the very source of meaning itself, and to do so in a way that engages the gathered community, is relevant to its lived context, and opens up the potential for transformation.

This book is about what happens when we let the stories of our lives intersect with the stories of our faith tradition, and the preaching that emerges at that crossroads – preaching that speaks in the present tense. Each chapter begins with a story in the life of the community. Some are personal, some are global. Some stories are new; others are old, surfaced by current events. An earthquake in Haiti. Residential schools for Indigenous children. *Star Wars*. Same-sex marriage. A pilgrimage on the Camino de Santiago. At first glance, the stories may have little in common. And yet, when put into conversation with the biblical text, they give birth to holy meaning and to an experience of the divine. That, at least, is the hope. We look for meaning in the serendipitous encounter of an ancient story and the present life of the community. Then, we speak.

1. Anna Carter Florence, *Preaching as Testimony* (Louisville: Westminster John Knox Press, 2007), xiii.
2. Thomas G. Long, *Preaching from Memory to Hope* (Louisville: Westminster John Knox Press, 2009), xv.

3. Here I follow the work of Charles Taylor, *A Secular Age* (Cambridge: Belknap Press, 2007), 25–27.

4. Karl Rahner, "Christian Living Formerly and Today," in *Theological Investigations VII*, trans. David Bourke (New York: Herder and Herder, 1971), 15, as quoted in Harvey D. Egan, *Soundings in the Christian Mystical Tradition* (Collegeville, MN: Liturgical Press, 2010), 338.

5. Paul Ricoeur, "The Hermeneutics of Testimony" in *Essays on Biblical Interpretation*, ed. Lewis Mudge (Philadelphia: Fortress Press, 1980), 128.

6. Barbara Brown Taylor, *The Preaching Life* (Cambridge: Cowley Publications, 1993), 77.

7. Thomas G. Long, *The Witness of Preaching* (Louisville: Westminster John Knox, 2005), 52.

8. Barbara Brown Taylor, *The Preaching Life*, 11.

ONE

Power in a Name

Eliot burst into my office. "I want to change my name."

"Haven't you already changed your name?"

"Yes, but now I want to do it legally, and I found this liturgy and I'm wondering if we could have a renaming at church," they[1] said, thrusting a book into my hands. Eliot's words were tumbling out in a rush, faster than usual. Clearly this mattered, and there was a look of expectancy as I turned my attention to the book: *Transgendering Faith: Identity, Sexuality and Spirituality.*[2] Eliot had marked the page, "'I Am' – A Liturgy of ReNaming for Transgender Persons."

I met Eliot in the summer of 2013 on a Sunday morning at St. Albans Church. But the first real hint of their story came later that summer at the Ottawa Pride Parade. Every year, a group from St. Albans walks in the parade. It's a statement, and it's also a lot of fun. Happy crowds line the streets, and plenty of colourful groups join the march. There are dancers and there are floats with powerful amplifiers pumping out the tunes. The church groups are among the least entertaining, but we still get big cheers, simply because we are there. Midway through the 2013 parade, someone raced out of the crowd onto the street, gave me a big hug, and then turned and ran back to their vantage point along the parade route. It was Eliot.

Eliot is a non-binary transgender person. They identify as neither male nor female. It's not easy being transgender in our society. We like to fit people into categories, and one of the categories that we regard as most important is whether you are male or female. For cisgender people – people whose gender identity is consistent with the gender they were assigned at birth – that's not a problem. For transgender people, it's a challenge. What washroom to use, how to dress, how to fill out forms, what name to use, looks of confusion or open hostility: all of these can be daunting and can lead to experiences of alienation and marginalization. Transitioning from one gender to another can be a rocky road, as one wrestles not only with one's own sense of identity, but also with the objections of family, the bewilderment of friends, scarce medical support, social harassment, and often violence.

For many of us, and for our churches, transgender identity is something new, and we don't understand it very well. But there are times when we have to respond even before we understand. At St. Albans, we are committed to welcoming anyone who enters our community. When Eliot took the courageous step of coming through our doors, they were embraced. And they, in turn, embraced us, joining our Student Internship Program and becoming one of the most active members of the congregation.

Eliot's prior church experience had been difficult, and resentment bubbled up once in a while. But despite, or maybe because of all that, Eliot became a much loved member of the congregation. One of our most moving moments as a community came two years later, when Eliot reflected on the story of Philip and the Ethiopian eunuch. The story describes the unlikely encounter between one of Jesus' disciples and a foreigner who has been marginalized from the worshipping community because of his sexuality. The story concludes with Philip baptizing the Ethiopian (Acts 8:26–39). Eliot told us that they were the eunuch, but that we had been their Philip.

So there was no question when Eliot came into my office that morning that our community wanted to support Eliot in particular and the transgender community in general. My initial instinct was to just go ahead and do it, to take the renaming liturgy that Eliot offered and to incorporate it into an upcoming Sunday service. But Eliot wasn't in a hurry. In fact their grandmother was coming to town in a couple of months, and Eliot thought it would be nice to do the renaming then. That gave us a bit of time to think.

There was the liturgy itself, which did a good job of drawing on scriptural examples of renaming, but which looked a little bit too much like a baptism. We could rework that part, substituting an anointing with oil for the water symbolism, a subtle reference to the healing power of what we would be doing. More importantly, though, Eliot and I agreed that rather than go ahead with the liturgy in an under-the-radar sort of way, we would do things properly, upping the ante in the process. In our tradition, that meant asking the bishop for permission for a trial use of the new liturgy, something that had the potential to make our exercise a learning experience for the church more broadly, and a more visible demonstration of support for the transgender community.

First, I spoke to my archdeacon, the senior priest in our area. He was enthusiastic and concurred that the time was right for the church to explore ministry to the transgender community in concrete ways. With his help and support, I sent the proposed liturgy of renaming to Bishop John, with a request for permission for a trial use at St. Albans. A positive response came back from the bishop's office in short order.

Meanwhile, Eliot and I had locked onto a date for the renaming. As it happened, the date coincided with the baptism of another of our university students named Davis. Because Davis wanted a full-immersion baptism, we would be doing part of the baptism liturgy in the church building and then the actual baptism in a nearby river. This was shaping up to be no ordinary Sunday morning, but I still hadn't fully grasped how extraordinary it would become. The planned renaming at St. Albans took on an even bigger significance for Eliot when their application for a legal name change was initially rejected by the government.

That Sunday morning the church was packed. Our community was out in full force to express its support for Eliot, and for Davis, and our ranks were supplemented by their families and friends. The congregation that day included a significant number of transgender people, some of whom were regulars in our community, some of whom probably hadn't set foot in a church for years, if ever. Anticipation filled the air. Later, a few people told me that they had the sense of being part of something epic, a historic moment. For their part, Eliot described it as their best week ever.

The assigned gospel reading for that Sunday was from Mark.

John said to him, "Teacher, we saw someone casting out demons in your name, and we tried to stop him, because he was not following us." But Jesus said, "Do not stop him; for no one who does a deed of power in my name will be able soon afterwards to speak evil of me. Whoever is not against us is for us" (Mark 9:38–40, NRSV).

SERMON

Power in a Name[3]

There is power in a name. In the gospel we just
heard, there is a man who is casting out demons in the name of
Jesus, a powerful act. This is a man who knows the power of Jesus'
name, who is doing good deeds in Jesus' name. But there seems to
be a problem. He's not one of "us": "Teacher we saw someone casting
out demons in your name, and we tried to stop him, because he was
not following us."

Today we will celebrate a naming. And we will celebrate a
renaming.

Davis is being baptized today. He wanted lots of water, so after
we are done here we will be heading to Mooney's Bay for his baptism.

Davis, from this day on, you will bear the name of Christ, which
literally means "the anointed one." We are going to go to the river,
submerge you in the waters, and bring you out again. It will be a
symbol and a sacrament of your baptism into the death and
resurrection of Christ, and of your new birth and new life. You will
be anointed with oil, and you will bear the name of Christ, the
anointed one, child of God. And, as one who bears the name of Christ,
you will from this day on act in the name of Jesus, and do mighty
deeds in Jesus' name.

There is power in a name.

Eliot, you too will be anointed today, just as you were anointed
at your own baptism many years ago. You continue to bear the name
of Christ, the anointed one, beloved child of God. We reaffirm that
name today. That has not changed. But some things *do* change.

Often our faith journeys can take twists and turns as we live and
grow into the people that God created us to be. Today you take on a
new name as a testimony to the person you have become and as a
testimony to the God who welcomes us as God's children, loves us

through all the twists and turns of our life journeys, and promises to make all things new.

There is power in a name.

There will be some who will wonder why we are celebrating a liturgy for the renaming of a transgender person at St. Albans today. There might be some who would wish to stop us, who think that this is not something that the church should be doing: "Jesus, we saw someone casting out demons in your name, and we tried to stop him because he was not following us."

"Because he was not following us." Did you notice the "us" in that complaint? The problem wasn't that the man wasn't following Jesus; the problem was that the man wasn't following *us*. He wasn't one of *us*; he wasn't doing things *our* way. One of the realities of our human condition is that we tend to think in terms of "us versus them." We are part of a group, or many groups. Those groups can be family groups, ethnic groups, religious groups, social groups – whatever. We tend to draw our identity from the groups to which we belong. And, sometimes, we strengthen our individual identities by strengthening our group identity, by drawing boundaries around our groups that allow us to know who is in and who is out. If an outsider wants to be part of our group, well, they will just have to play by our rules.

People who are queer or transgender in our society and in our church understand this dynamic all too well. They know first-hand the barriers and boundaries that we set up to define who is in and who is out.

"Jesus, we tried to stop him because he was not following us."

And Jesus replies, "Do not stop him."

There is a fundamental generosity in Jesus' response, a generosity that transcends all of our us-versus-them boundaries and barriers. It is a gracious generosity, an inclusive generosity, a compassionate generosity, a generosity that offers a cup of water to any and all who thirst.

Some people resist that generosity, perhaps because they are afraid that it means that "anything goes." But of course it doesn't. Clearly that's not what Jesus means – certainly not in today's gospel. Jesus goes on to say that if anyone puts a stumbling block in the way of someone who believes in him, it would be better to put a millstone around that person's neck and throw them into the sea. He goes on to say that if your foot causes you to stumble, better to cut it off and enter life lame than to have two feet and be thrown into hell. That certainly doesn't sound like "anything goes" to me. *How* we live matters, and there are right ways and wrong ways to go about it. There are right ways and wrong ways to treat each other. Discipleship, the call to follow Jesus, is a demanding call; it is a call to take up your cross, to love God, and to love your neighbour.

But discipleship is also a call to a fundamental generosity and graciousness that transcends the human boundaries and barriers we ourselves create with our us-versus-them mentality. The scriptures attest to this. We find again and again that the moments when God's grace surprises and confounds humanity are the very moments when that grace is more generous than we could have imagined and when it crosses boundaries that we thought could not be crossed. Jesus eats with outcasts and sinners, confounding the rule-makers of his time. He is convinced by the Syrophoenician woman to extend his ministry to foreigners, not just to the Jewish people. The early church, in a powerful movement of the Holy Spirit, breaks with tradition so that Gentiles may be fully included in the body of Christ.

To borrow a phrase from "This Holy Estate: The Report of the Commission on the Marriage Canon of the Anglican Church of Canada," in all these moments in scripture, "there is a recognition that God's grace is broader than we had assumed, and that those who had been excluded are now being invited in."[4]

And so to those who ask why we are celebrating a liturgy of renaming for a transgender person today, I would humbly answer that it is because Jesus wants us to show a generosity to all God's children that transcends and breaks down the us-versus-them boundaries and barriers that exist in our church and in our society.

Also, it's because we love you, Eliot.

The truth is, I may never be able to understand what it's like to be a non-binary transgender person. But, at least in our better moments, by the grace of God, we are able to be generous by offering our support to a fellow traveller who bears the name of Christ on their faith journey.

We will walk with you.

1. They/them are Eliot's preferred pronouns.
2. Leanne McCall & Maren C. Tirabassi, editors, *Transgendering Faith: Identity, Sexuality and Spirituality*. (Cleveland: Pilgrim Press, 2004).
3. Sermon: Sept 27, 2015. Readings: Esther 7:1–6, 9–10, 9:20, 22; Psalm 124; James 5:13–20; Mark 9:38–50.
4. "This Holy Estate: The Report of the Commission on the Marriage Canon of the Anglican Church of Canada," September 2015, www.anglican.ca/wp-content/uploads/Marriage_Canon_REPORT_15Sept22.pdf (accessed March 4, 2017).

TWO

Witness among the Stones

I recently spent an evening at a retreat centre in suburban Toronto in the company of preachers from across Canada. We were there for a preaching workshop, but that evening our preaching was put on hold and politics took over. It was the night of the American presidential election. We set up a big screen in one of the conference rooms and gathered to watch as the results trickled in. At first the colours on the map were encouraging. By 11:30 pm, I'd seen enough. It was getting late, and though I was tempted to keep watching, I'd worked through enough combinations of state-by-state results to declare for myself what the big networks hadn't yet dared to pronounce. Donald Trump was going to be the next president of the United States of America.

As a Canadian, I'd watched the Trump phenomenon from a distance. Initially, it was entertaining, like one of those reality TV shows that you don't really want to watch but that keeps drawing you in. At first, it was hard to believe that Americans were taking him seriously, so it was easy to laugh at his outbursts and to take it all with a grain of salt. When he secured the Republican nomination, it became disturbing. The dystopian vision put forward in his speech at the Republican National Convention, stoking the fears of a nation that was already clearly divided, was ominous. It only got worse as the lying, the misogyny, and the scapegoating of Muslims and

Mexicans became more pronounced, but all the experts thought that Hillary Clinton was going to win. And then she didn't. Suddenly, the geographical and psychological distance that insulates Canadians from the vagaries of American election campaigns collapsed.

The next morning, I went to the cafeteria to join our group of 30 or so for breakfast. Many people were upset, but none more so than the Americans in our midst who'd been fearing this outcome for months. For most of us, the election result felt like a betrayal of our values and many expressed concerns about what would come next. The gospel reading for the coming Sunday was apocalyptic, and it captured something of the mood of our group.

When some were speaking about the temple, how it was adorned with beautiful stones and gifts dedicated to God, Jesus said, "As for these things that you see, the days will come when not one stone will be left upon another; all will be thrown down." They asked him, "Teacher, when will this be, and what will be the sign that this is about to take place?" And he said, "Beware that you are not led astray; for many will come in my name and say, 'I am he!' and, 'The time is near!' Do not go after them.

"When you hear of wars and insurrections, do not be terrified; for these things must take place first, but the end will not follow immediately." Then he said to them, "Nation will rise against nation, and kingdom against kingdom; there will be great earthquakes, and in various places famines and plagues; and there will be dreadful portents and great signs from heaven. But before all this occurs, they will arrest you and persecute you; they will hand you over to synagogues and prisons, and you will be brought before kings and governors because of my name. This will give you an opportunity to testify" (Luke 21:5–13, NRSV).

SERMON

Witness among the Stones[1]

"Look at these great stones!"

My tour guide pointed at the temple wall in Jerusalem. Massive stones weighing as much as 80 tonnes towered above us. We marvelled at their size and grandeur.

We love great stones. The temple in Jerusalem. The pyramids in Egypt. The Great Wall of China. All of them testaments to human ingenuity and engineering. All of them major tourist destinations. All of them admired for their size and beauty. All of them testaments to human terror. The fear of invasion. The fear of death. The fear that God will forsake us.

Because when earthquakes, famines, and plagues occur; when humans arrest, persecute, and betray one another; when families are divided; when war and insurrections happen – and these things happen in every age – we are terrified. And we respond with stones.

Not far from where Jesus' disciples stood, admiring the great stones of the temple, there are more stones. There is a wall that passes near to Jerusalem and extends more than 700 kilometres to keep Palestinians out of Israel. When we are afraid, we build walls. Barbed wire fences to keep Syrian refugees out of Europe. A wall on the border with Mexico. We want to control things – we need to keep people out – because we are afraid.

We love great stones. Armies and weapons. Governments and institutions. The United Nations and NATO. Trade agreements and border protection. All great stones. All designed to protect us from the things that terrify us: wars and insurrections, conflict and terrorism.

We pile up stones in our bank accounts and in our pensions. In our homes, fences, and gates. We are led astray by false prophets and we go after them in search of prosperity and security – nationalism, tribalism, consumerism, escapism, name your "ism."

Jesus says, "As for these things you see, the days will come when not one stone will be left upon another; all will be thrown down."

Yes, there will be wars and insurrection. Yes, there will be earthquakes and plagues. Yes, families will be divided. Yes, people will be arrested and persecuted. And yes, sooner or later these things will touch you and those that you love.

And there will be false prophets who offer solutions. Strong leaders who identify enemies and scapegoats. Demagogues who would suspend civil rights "to make us safe." Beware that you are not led astray. Do not be terrified. Because if you are terrified, you too will respond with stones.

Do not be afraid, for you have another calling.

You have been called to be a witness. Especially in troubled times, when stones are being piled up and thrown down, God has called you to a particular vocation. You will be given the opportunity to testify.

You may not think at first that the opportunity to testify is much of a gift. In fact, if wars and insurrections don't scare you, the thought that you're supposed to testify just might!

But testimony is who we *are* as disciples of Jesus. In his very last words before his ascension, Jesus said, "You will be my witnesses in Jerusalem, throughout Judea and Samaria, and to the ends of the earth."

Witness. Testify. That's what we are called to do as followers of Jesus, as God's people in the world. It is our vocation. And what a gift it is to be given the opportunity to do the very thing that God has called us to do. To become the people that God has called us to be. To be God's witnesses.

To testify, to give witness – these are images drawn from the courts of law. A witness is someone who has seen something important about the matter at hand, and then speaks truthfully to the court about what he or she has seen.

For many people, when life is hard, when there are wars and deaths and disasters, the matter at hand is this: Where is God in all of this? Is there a God at all?

If the evidence of our eyes and ears suggests that God is absent, or that there is no God, then we look for other solutions, and we become afraid, and we respond with stones.

But yours is the voice that says no, that says that God is still here in the midst of all this pain. You are the one who can look into the storms of life, see God at work – healing, comforting, inspiring, redeeming – and then tell us what you have seen. That's what witnesses do. That's what it means to testify.

You don't need to prepare your testimony in advance. You can't! You don't know yet what you will see, where you will see God in the storms that are coming from beyond the horizon. But here Jesus offers us another gift – the assurance that when the time comes, and the time *is* coming, he will give us the words and wisdom that we will need to speak.

What we need to do, starting now, is to put our trust in God and be ready to share the hope that lives within us. And our hope is this: we are an Easter people. We have seen Jesus crucified and raised from the dead and so we are not afraid in times of trouble, because we know that even in death we will be raised by the power of God. Of this we are witnesses. We are the ones who are convinced that neither death nor life – not rulers, not powers, not anything in all of creation – will be able to separate us from the love of God.

Now, I'm not claiming that this testimony thing is easy. It's not. The gospel text today does not suggest that everything will be easy. In fact, quite the opposite is true. I've spent most of this week wrestling with testimony. I was in Toronto for several days participating in a preaching workshop with Anna Carter Florence. She has written a book called *Preaching as Testimony*. Our job as preachers, she says, is to go into the text – the bit of scripture we've been given to preach on – to engage with it, wrestle with it, poke it and prod it, and to let it poke us and prod us; to stay there and not come back until we've seen something that is true, something true and of God. And only *then* are we to return and tell others what we've seen. That's how I, as a preacher, do testimony; I engage the text, enter into it, struggle with it, wrestle with it until I see something true about us and about God, and then I come here on Sunday and tell you what I see.

You, as a disciple of Jesus, as one who has been given the vocation of witness, you too are called to testify. As a preacher, I am given a text from scripture. But your text is your life. Every day you have the opportunity to engage life, to enter into it, to struggle with it, to pray with it, to wrestle with it until you see something that is true about God. Then, you tell others what you see. We can do this. God will provide the opportunity, the words and the wisdom.

In today's gospel reading, Jesus points to challenging times ahead. It is especially during times of trouble that God needs witnesses, that *all* of us need witnesses who can speak God's truth. Who can testify to God's redeeming love, present and active in the world. Who can reassure us that we can trust in God and that God is good.

When life gets hard, many will respond with stones. But we are called to testify.

1. Sermon: November 13, 2016. Readings: Isaiah 65:17–25; Isaiah 12; 2 Thessalonians 3:6–13; Luke 21:5–19.

THREE

I Will Not
Keep Silent

Serious voices spoke from the overhead screen as I walked into the bar to join my hockey buddies. It was the second Tuesday of the month, our usual get-together at the pub. Most nights we could expect to see a hockey game on the television, but tonight there were talking heads interspersed with scenes of crumbled buildings. I was feeling a bit cranky.

"Oh look, another natural disaster somewhere in the world to fill up airtime on CNN," I muttered.

My hockey buddy, a journalist, turned to me: "This isn't just another natural disaster. It's big."

He was right, though at that moment I didn't appreciate how right he was. It had only been four hours since a massive earthquake had shaken the island nation of Haiti, its epicentre just 25 kilometres west of the capital of Port-au-Prince. The initial images coming out of the country only hinted at the extent of the devastation that had been wreaked. Buildings demolished. Entire villages flattened. Every hospital in Port-au-Prince severely damaged or destroyed. People sleeping in the open, fearful of frequent aftershocks. An impoverished people in a desolate land clinging to survival.

Even before the earthquake hit, Haiti, with its ten million inhabitants, was the poorest country in the Western Hemisphere. That poverty was not simply the result of geography and misfortune.

Since the arrival of Columbus in 1492, Haiti and its people have endured 500 years of colonization, occupation, and corrupt governance. As an article in *The Guardian* newspaper reported, "Haiti has had slavery, revolution, debt, deforestation, corruption, exploitation and violence. Now it has poverty, illiteracy, overcrowding, no infrastructure, environmental disaster and large areas without the rule of law. And that was before the earthquake."[1]

Three million people were directly affected by the disaster – some buried, many more clinging to survival, lacking food, water, and shelter. Eventually the death toll reached well over 100,000.

The international response was immediate. Search and rescue teams scrambled to look through the rubble for survivors. Canadian military personnel were dispatched. Naval ships sailed to towns and villages to which road access had been blocked by debris. The Canadian government sent financial aid and set up a matching fund for individual donations to the relief effort. NGOs and charities directed their field staff to the hardest-hit areas. Journalists flooded into Haiti with their cameras and satellite links.

The earthquake in Haiti penetrated our collective consciousness in a way not seen since the 2004 Boxing Day tsunami in the Indian Ocean. Perhaps it was the constant stream of images, video, and news. Maybe it was because of the large Haitian diaspora found in Montreal and, to a lesser extent, in Ottawa. Whatever the reason, the event felt close to home and we were compelled to help. We believed we could help. We engaged – individually and as communities. That engagement manifested itself in a variety of ways. There was a surge of compassion and a desire to do something, which, for many of us, took the form of financial donations. But there were also conversations and reflections that went deep, confronted as we were by daily images of life and death. The tragic images on our screens clashed with the comfort of our living rooms.

In faith communities and beyond, tragedy and dissonance give rise to questions. Why Haiti? Could it happen here? How does this earthquake fit with my understanding of creation? Why would God let this happen? Where is God in the midst of suffering? As communities of faith, we are vulnerable in moments such as these. Our compassion for those who suffer draws us, at least in some measure, into their pain. At the same time, our reason brings once more to the fore the hard questions that we usually keep off to the side. Sometimes it seems the only answer we are given is silence.

Maybe that's why, when I looked at the scriptures we would read on Sunday, the following words jumped out at me: "I will not keep silent."

What does it mean to break the silence? To dare to put forward an answer – or maybe not even an "answer" – but at least to open our mouths in response to the existential questions of our lives, which are so often answered with silence? How would the preachers in Haiti break the silence on that Sunday morning, knowing as they must how the devastation around them would challenge the faith and drain the hope of a devout people? And how are we to respond from our place of comfort?

The first reading for that Sunday was from the prophet Isaiah, from the sixth century B.C. The people of Israel, who had been in exile in Babylon for 50 years, were finally allowed to return home to the city of Jerusalem. But when they arrived, they found the city in ruins, utterly destroyed. A deep silence fell upon the land. Then the prophet Isaiah broke the silence.

For Zion's sake I will not keep silent, and for Jerusalem's sake I will not rest, until her vindication shines out like the dawn, and her salvation like a burning torch. The nations shall see your vindication, and all the kings your glory; and you shall be called by a new name that the mouth of the Lord will give. You shall be a crown of beauty in the hand of the Lord, and a royal diadem in the hand of your God (Isaiah 62:1–3, NRSV).

In contrast, the gospel was about a celebration, a wedding feast.

On the third day there was a wedding in Cana of Galilee, and the mother of Jesus was there. Jesus and his disciples had also been invited to the wedding. When the wine gave out, the mother of Jesus said to him, "They have no wine." And Jesus said to her, "Woman, what concern is that to you and to me? My hour has not yet come." His mother said to the servants, "Do whatever he tells you." Now standing there were six stone water jars for the Jewish rites of purification, each holding twenty or thirty gallons. Jesus said to them, "Fill the jars with water." And they filled them up to the brim... (John 2:1–8, NRSV).

SERMON

I Will Not Keep Silent[2]

I will not keep silent. These are the words of the prophet Isaiah, in today's Old Testament reading, as he stands in the midst of the people in the ruined city of Jerusalem.

The people of Jerusalem had been forced into exile in Babylon when the Babylonian army had defeated the city and destroyed it in 587 B.C. A generation later, the exiled people had been given new hope when the Persian Empire defeated the Babylonians and the Persian king, Cyrus, had decreed that the people of Israel would be allowed to return home.

But they had no idea what would be waiting for them when they arrived back in Jerusalem. Jerusalem had been destroyed. Buildings had collapsed, there was no water supply, the ground was dry, the city was in ruins. An impoverished people had returned to a desolate land. They felt that God had forsaken them. A deafening silence fell over the land.

One of the first newspaper articles that I read this week about Haiti, in the immediate aftermath of the earthquake, reported that an unnerving silence had replaced the normal sounds of the city of Port-au-Prince. Silence, punctuated by the occasional lament, is the sound of desperation, the sound of desolation and forsakenness. Silence is the sound of a people in need of salvation.

Into Jerusalem's devastation, the prophet's voice cries out, "I will not keep silent, I will not rest until this people is vindicated and their salvation shines out like a burning torch, and they shall no more be called forsaken and desolate."

The prophet calls on the people to remember God's promises. The prophet calls on *God* to remember God's promises – the promise to be a refuge in times of trouble; to rescue the people of Israel; to be their salvation. This is a voice of hope. This is a voice of faith.

There was an interview on the radio with a Canadian

policewoman who had served recently in Haiti. At the end of the interview, she concluded her remarks by saying, "I pray that the people of Haiti, who are a deeply religious people, are able to keep their faith in the midst of this tragedy."

The cruel dilemma posed by tragic events is that just when we need our faith the most, it is severely challenged by the depth of suffering we encounter and by the questions and doubts that result. At this very moment, there are Haitians gathered in worship, not in church buildings, which lie in ruins, but in fields and streets and in whatever open space they can find. Many of them will be praying, singing, and listening to the same readings we just heard. Some, when they hear the miraculous story of Jesus turning water into wine, may be filled with hope. Others may think bitterly that if Jesus could turn water into wine, why couldn't he do something to prevent this earthquake?

From our safe vantage point, we need to recognize that this disaster in Haiti is not just a natural disaster, but also a disaster of human making. If this same earthquake had struck in a rich country, the death toll would likely be closer to 100 than the current estimate of 100,000. We have developed our global society in such a way that there are over a billion people living in extreme poverty, and that includes almost everyone in Haiti. It is humanity's willingness to tolerate poverty and injustice that sets the stage for the devastation we see playing out on our televisions. Not individually, but collectively, we are the ones who are responsible.

At these times we can also acknowledge that the universe was brought into being as a dynamic place that is still in the process of creation, and that this ongoing creation incorporates elements of change and destruction. The same movements in the earth's crust that allowed humanity to come into existence in the first place will cause earthquakes that take human life. Our death creates the opportunity for new generations to be born. God has declared creation good, although from our vantage point there are times when it doesn't appear that way.

What does all this do to our faith, to our faith in God's promises? Will you and I, like the prophet, refuse to keep silent and instead proclaim the promise of salvation, even in the midst of tragedy?

It helps if we pay close attention to what God has actually promised. God *hasn't* promised that there will *never* be times of trouble. God has promised to be our *refuge* in times of trouble. God doesn't promise that we will *never* need to be rescued. God *does* promise to rescue us. God *never* promised that we won't need salvation. God has promised to be our saviour.

When we suffer, when we encounter tragedy, God suffers with us. And not only does God suffer with us, God enters into our tragedy and seeks to transform our sadness into joy. This may not be a painless process, it may not be immediate, but this is the promise that we are given. In the midst of the desolation of Jerusalem, the prophet Isaiah breaks the silence and proclaims this promise to the people. I pray that, at this very moment, these same promises are being proclaimed to the people of Haiti as they gather in worship, and that they are able to keep their faith in the midst of this tragedy.

But declaring the promises of God is not enough. The prophet goes on to say, "I will not rest until the people have been saved." God has promised to enter into our tragedies and to transform sadness into joy. But how do you think that's going to happen? It happens, at least in part, through us. *We* are called to participate in God's promise to be a refuge for those in trouble, to rescue those in need, and to bring salvation to all people.

There is no mystery about what salvation looks like at this very moment in Port-au-Prince. Salvation looks like a jug of clean drinking water, a bag of food, shelter, and medical services. We have a role to play if God's presence and loving kindness are to be made known to the people of Haiti. For that reason I commend the actions of our government and of the many people who are contributing generously to the relief efforts, and I encourage all of you to get involved and to uphold the people of Haiti in your prayers.

At one level, today's gospel story of the wedding at Cana seems a bit trivial compared to a natural disaster. After all, running out of wine at a wedding can hardly be called a national emergency. But at a deeper level, the transformation of water into wine is something that John calls a "sign." It is symbolic of God's deep desire to transform human sorrow into joy. This is a deeply symbolic story that gives us a glimpse of what God is like.

There is much that could be said about this text, but there is one detail in the story that I want to draw attention to this morning. That detail is found in the role of the servants in the story. The servants certainly don't have all the answers, nor are they able to change water into wine. But they play an important role. When Jesus asks them to fill the pots with water, not only do they do it, but, we're told, they fill them to the brim. The part that they are given to play in God's great transformation of sorrow into joy, they fulfill with enthusiasm and to the very best of their abilities.

It is our privilege that we have been asked to participate in the realization of God's promises in our world. We are all given a part to play. When God asks you to fill the jar with water, will you fill it to the brim? And can you say with the prophet, "I will not keep silent and I will not rest until the people have been saved"?

1. Alex von Tunzelmann, a historian and writer, quoted in *The Guardian*, January 14, 2010. www.theguardian.com/world/2010/jan/14/haiti-history-earthquake-disaster (accessed March 4, 2017).
2. Sermon: Jan 17, 2010. Readings: Isaiah 62:1–5; John 2:1–11.

FOUR

Where You Put Your Body

As the last shovelful of gravel crunched into the wheelbarrow, I found myself thinking about incarnation. A construction site in rural Nicaragua might seem an odd place for theological reflection, but with sweat pouring off my nose and strained muscles protesting their unaccustomed use, I was fully aware of my embodied state. We had travelled south to build a school in the tiny village of Bella Vista – 16 of us in total, nine teens and seven adults. The genesis of the trip was an encounter between Tom and our teenagers in the parish of Huntley. Our teens connected with Tom. He was young enough to be of their generation, but old enough to be making his mark: the local kid from the village down the road with a story to tell. Tom relayed to a captivated audience how he, as a new university graduate, had desperately wanted to make a difference in the world. But he also remembered feeling as if he had little to offer, and his attempt to begin a career in international development just didn't seem to be going anywhere. Overwhelmed, and disillusioned, he travelled to Nicaragua. In a village in the northern part of the country, not far from Bella Vista, he met a little girl and, on impulse, gave her his notebook and a pencil. The girl disappeared, but a few moments later she came back with her father, and the man had tears in his eyes. "Thank you so much," he said. "Now my daughter can go to school this year." In her village, a child can only go to school if she can bring her own school supplies, and this girl's family was one of many who could not afford them.

The encounter changed Tom's life. Inspired, he decided to start a small charitable organization dedicated to helping kids in Nicaragua go to school. He did his homework and, before long, with the support of friends and family in his hometown of Almonte, SchoolBox was born. It was seven years later that Tom would meet with us in Carp to tell us about the work of SchoolBox in Nicaragua. The enterprise, which began with the provision of school supplies, soon grew to include the construction of school buildings, and volunteer groups were being organized and sent to participate in the school-building projects. Captivated by Tom's story, our teenagers were ready to board the next flight to Managua.

Of course, it wasn't quite as simple as that. A trip to Nicaragua to build a school would require planning and fundraising. But it would also involve education and preparation to put it all in context. I was very aware of the perils of church mission trips and of "voluntourism" in general: the risk of a smug do-gooder mentality, the lack of cultural context, the waste of funds, the entrenchment of stereotypes, the exploitation of those we think we are helping. But Tom and the rest of the folks at SchoolBox seemed to be well aware of those pitfalls. With some careful planning, and with some honesty up front about who the real beneficiaries of our trip would be (ourselves!), we thought we could structure an enriching and potentially transformative experience for our teens that would, at the same time, assist SchoolBox in its work and benefit the Nicaraguans with whom we would be working. One year later, we boarded our flight to Managua.

After a long travel day, we were up bright and early the next morning, ready to load into a couple of vans for the long and bumpy drive to Bella Vista. Upon arrival, the whole village was there to welcome us. They'd created a colourful arch of balloons for us to walk through as we arrived on site. The existing classroom was a small thatched structure that leaked during the long rainy season.

Nearby was the one-room concrete building that we would be completing. The village school children made us feel at home in an instant. Tom was there too. After a few hours of mixing concrete and digging toilet pits under the watchful gaze of the Nicaraguan construction foreman, Tom gathered us together. He gave us some practical advice, such as the need to take frequent breaks, reapply sunscreen, and drink lots of fluids in the hot weather. More importantly, he reminded us that the main reason we were there was not to provide manual labour on a construction site, but to love the kids in the community. That was a mission our young people took to heart, and so we took regular breaks from work to play with the Nicaraguan children. The water cooler area became the place where games started. And, when the breaks were over and work began again, the village children worked right alongside us, shovelling gravel and wheeling cement, and having a great time as they helped to build their own school. We got to know one another despite the language barrier.

Tom was right about why we were there. As construction workers, eager but unskilled, we could be replaced by Nicaraguan labour for a few dollars a day. But the relationships we were building were priceless. The work was important, because it showed that we cared, and that we believed in what the community was doing. As Tom pointed out to me later that evening, the most difficult thing in Nicaragua isn't the construction of schools, it's motivating the children and their families to *stay* in school. The fact that our teens were there working hard to build the school showed that they cared about education. That would help. As would the wheelbarrow rides, soccer games, and water fights. The balloons were fitting. The whole construction site took on something of a party atmosphere.

I found myself thinking about incarnation. In some ways, our journey to Nicaragua had become a metaphor for the incarnation. Why did God become flesh and dwell among us? Couldn't God have just done his thing "long-distance"? Was it really necessary to put feet on the ground, to suffer, to love, to do all those bodily things that are the essence of our existence?

Why did we travel to Nicaragua? Was it really necessary to show up in Bella Vista in the flesh? After all, we could have stayed at home and just sent the money to build the school. But instead we chose to put our feet on the ground in the village. Did it make a difference to the people there? You bet it did! We could see it in their faces, in their smiles, in their hospitality. On site, we worked hard, we played hard, we sweated, and we ached at the end of each day. We had skin in the game. Our presence, our willingness to build a school for these kids, with these kids, showed them that we cared. That was the foundation upon which we built relationships. Being there changed us, and it changed them. It matters where we put our bodies.

Theologians call that incarnation.

Our last day in Nicaragua was a Sunday. Our project was complete. The school had been built and blessed, and inaugurated by local officials. We had a church service at the hotel in Leon, outside by the swimming pool. The scripture passage I chose for our worship together was one that we usually reserve for Christmas, the prologue from the Gospel of John.

In the beginning was the Word, and the Word was with God, and the Word was God. The Word was in the beginning with God. All things came into being through the Word, and without the Word not one thing came into being. What has come into being in the Word was life, and the life was the light of all people. The light shines in the darkness, and the darkness did not overcome it...

And the Word became flesh and lived among us and we have seen his glory, the glory as of a parent's only son, full of grace and truth (John 1:1–5, 14, *NRSV* adapted).

It was nine months later that these words would be read once more at church back home, on Christmas Eve. It was again time to think about incarnation.

SERMON

Where You Put Your Body[1]

How many of you have been present for the birth of a child? Do you remember what it was like? Of course you do. The excitement, the nervousness, the sounds and smells of the birthing place. The overwhelming sense of joy when the child is born. Hearing those words, "It's a girl" or "It's a boy." For those of us who have had the privilege of being there, it is a peak experience, an event that fills us with joy and that sends us running to share the good news, by phone and email and social media, in words and in pictures, with friends, family, and even with complete strangers.

We use the image of the birth of a child each year as a way of capturing the joy and wonder of Christmas, the good news that was proclaimed by the angels to the shepherds in the fields near Bethlehem, the good news that was proclaimed by the prophet Isaiah so many years before that. For 2,000 years, we have proclaimed that the baby wrapped in swaddling clothes and lying in a manger was the Word who was God, who became flesh and lived among us.

When you think about it, that's a big claim. And there have, of course, been those who have disagreed with that claim over the centuries. One of the objections voiced by those who call themselves philosophers is this: Why would God, the almighty creator of the heavens and the earth, why would this God want to be born, choose to be born, as a tiny, vulnerable human being? Whatever it was that God hoped to achieve – peace, forgiveness, reconciliation, renewal, whatever it was – couldn't God, being God, have done it some other way? Perhaps in a way that was a little more dignified, a little more, well, more Godlike?

When I returned to school to study theology a few years back, I put this question to one of my professors at the seminary. "Why the incarnation?" I asked him. "Why did God become human in the person of Jesus and dwell on earth with us? Couldn't God have just done things long-distance?" My professor was an older man, past retirement age but still teaching. And he looked at me with the experience and wisdom that comes from all those years, and he said quite simply, "Son, it matters where you put your body."

"It matters where you put your body." His words reminded me of a pearl of wisdom spoken by another sage named Woody Allen, who once said, "Eighty percent of life is just showing up."

On that first Christmas day, God showed up. He took on a human body and put that body on this earth and was born a babe in Bethlehem. Does that make a difference?

I think it *does* matter where you put your body. It matters to people whether you show up or not. In my life, I've experienced this most clearly at weddings and funerals. I've found that it really matters to people whether you show up, whether you put your body in that pew or chair. I'm not sure I understand why. But even if I hardly get to talk to anybody, even if I don't get to express my congratulations or condolences, the very fact of showing up matters, more than sending gifts or flowers. There is no substitute for being there.

During the March break of this year, I took a group of high school students to Nicaragua to build a school in a rural area. We spent a year preparing for the trip, fundraising, learning about Nicaragua, learning about poverty and issues of development and social justice, learning about how all of this fits with our faith.

When we arrived in Nicaragua, we were met by Tom, the president of SchoolBox, the NGO that organized the school build and the trip. During that initial briefing, Tom told us something very valuable. He said to us, "You think that you've come here to build a school, and you have. We'll be spending a week in the village, on the construction site, and you'll mix concrete and haul gravel and bend rebar and do all the hard work required to finish the school. But never forget, the main reason that you're here is to love the kids of the village, the ones who will be going to that school. You're here to care for them and to inspire those children."

And so, during that week, our teenagers worked hard, but

they also took time to play with the children of the village, to talk to them in fractured Spanish, to see their homes and to play their games, and, when we worked, the children of the village worked alongside us.

At the end of our trip, the school was built. We gathered as a group, and we had a debriefing. I said to the teens, "During this past week we built a school. But you know, we could have done that long distance. We could have stayed in Canada and sent the money here to Nicaragua, and SchoolBox could have hired local labourers to do all the work that we did. But instead we chose to come here, to show up, to put our bodies here and do it in the flesh. Did that make a difference?"

And here's what those nine teenagers told me.

They told me that being there had been our way of showing the Nicaraguans that we cared; that it was an expression of love and solidarity. They told me that it allowed them and the people of the village to get to know each other; to play, to work, and to laugh together. They told me that we'd built trust together. They told me that they thought they had inspired the Nicaraguan children to continue with their schooling, and that the Nicaraguan children had inspired *them* to make a difference with their lives. They told me that they had built relationships – relationships that taught *them* things, relationships that transformed how they saw themselves and the world.

It matters where you put your body. It's important to show up. I think that's why the Word who was in the beginning, who was with God, who was God, became flesh and dwelt among us.

God showed up. Why? So that we could see and know God. As John wrote, the Word became flesh and lived among us and we have seen God's glory. No one has ever seen God. But we have seen Jesus, the Word become flesh, the one who is the very image of God, and it is he who has made God known.

God showed up in order to speak to us. As the writer to the Hebrews tells us, for thousands of years, God had been trying to communicate in many and various ways with humanity, with our ancestors, with limited success. But in these days, God has done something new: God has spoken to us through a son.

God speaks, in a way we can understand – in human language, in word and action, with facial expressions and hand movements and bodily gestures. But for communication to actually take place, we have to hear, we have to listen, we have to receive what is said. And, when we do, *then* we enter into relationship, a relationship with someone who cared enough to show up. To all who receive the Word, God gives power to become the children of God.

A few years ago, I spent three months in the Seychelles Islands as an intern, as part of my theological training. To get ready for that posting, I took part in a ten-day orientation program in Toronto. The program was for people from all over North America who were going overseas to do various types of work for the church. It was a great group of people, from many different backgrounds and with a lot of interesting stories to tell.

I remember one man from Texas, in particular. He was tall and slim, and he had the usual Texan accent, greeting us with a "Howdy y'all" when he entered the room. My Texan friend didn't talk a lot, he was a fairly quiet guy. But as we were going through the sessions and various exercises, whenever he *did* speak, he almost always said the same thing: "It's all about relationship." If we did a Bible study, invariably at some point he would chime in "Well, y'all know, it's all about relationship." If we did a session on how to work in a culture we weren't familiar with, he'd say, "Well, it's all about relationship." If we were getting training on issues of poverty or justice, same thing. And y'all know what? My Texan friend was always right.

And if he'd been sitting here with us today, and he'd heard today's gospel being read, and if we could ask him what he thought about it, I know what he would say. "It's all about relationship." And once more, he'd be right.

1. Sermon: Christmas Eve 2011. Readings: Isaiah 52:7–10; Psalm 98; Hebrews 1:1–4; John 1:1–18.

FIVE

Surely We're Not Blind, Are We?

"For the child taken, for the parent left behind."

It is the gaping wound in the soul of our country. For over a century, the government of Canada operated a system of residential schools for Indigenous children. More than 150,000 First Nations, Métis, and Inuit children were removed from their families and forced to attend these institutions, often far from their homes. Why? The Truth and Reconciliation Commission (TRC) – established by the Canadian government in 2008 to reveal the history and the ongoing legacy of the residential schools – reported the following:

These residential schools were created for the purpose of separating Aboriginal children from their families, in order to minimize and weaken family ties and cultural linkages, and to indoctrinate children into a new culture – the culture of the legally dominant Euro-Christian Canadian society, led by Canada's first prime minister, Sir John A. Macdonald.[1]

In 1883, Prime Minister Macdonald spoke to the House of Commons, to justify the government's residential school policy:

"When the school is on the reserve the child lives with its parents, who are savages; he is surrounded by savages, and though he may learn to read and write, his habits and training and mode of thought are Indian. He is simply a savage who can read and write. It has been strongly pressed on myself, as the head of the Department, that Indian children should be withdrawn as much as possible from the parental influence, and the only way to do that would be to put them in central training industrial schools where they will acquire the habits and modes of thought of white men."[2]

Canadian churches were complicit in the operation of the residential school system. First established in the 19th century, many of the residential schools were run by the Roman Catholic, Anglican, United, Methodist, and Presbyterian churches. Their partnership with the Canadian government lasted until 1969. Most of the schools were closed by the 1980s, though the last federally supported residential schools remained in operation until the mid-1990s.

According to the TRC, the main goal of the schools was not education, but rather to break the link between Indigenous children and their culture and identity. For these children, the cost was high. They were separated from their parents and communities. Many were abused, physically and sexually. Death rates in the residential schools were higher than would be tolerated in any other Canadian school system.

For children, life in these schools was lonely and alien. Buildings were poorly located, poorly built, and poorly maintained. The staff was limited in numbers, often poorly trained, and not adequately supervised. Many schools were poorly heated and poorly ventilated, and the diet was meagre and of poor quality. Discipline was harsh, and daily life was highly regimented. Aboriginal languages and cultures were denigrated and suppressed. The educational goals of the schools were limited and confused, and usually reflected a low regard for the intellectual capabilities of Aboriginal people.[3]

Though Canada's Indigenous policy, of which the residential school system was a central element, did not succeed in its original goal of eliminating Indigenous culture, the school system *did* do tremendous damage to the culture and the people, not just to the children taken into residential schools, but also to their families and descendants. The TRC concluded that the establishment and operation of residential schools was a key part of Canada's Aboriginal policy, "which can best be described as 'cultural genocide.'"

The Anglican Church of Canada's role in residential schools ended in 1969. But it was only when survivors' stories started coming out in the decades that followed – including accounts of sexual and physical abuse and the impact of the loss of culture – that the damage done by residential schools started to penetrate the public consciousness of non-Indigenous people in Canada. In 1993, the Primate of the Anglican Church of Canada, Michael Peers, issued a full apology for the church's role in the system and for the wrongs committed.

"I am sorry, more than I can say, that we were part of a system which took you and your children from home and family. I am sorry, more than I can say, that we tried to remake you in our image, taking from you your language and the signs of your identity. I am sorry, more than I can say, that in our schools so many were abused physically, sexually, culturally and emotionally. On behalf of the Anglican Church of Canada, I present our apology."[4]

All this hit home for me in a visceral, personal way during a visit in 2007 to a church near the site of a former residential school. It was the year that I would be travelling to the Seychelles Islands for an internship. As part of my orientation training, we went to visit a chapel in an Indigenous community. Our host, an Iroquois woman, explained the history of the beautiful building and gave us a guided tour. She spoke of historic events and of royal visits. Prompted by a few of our questions and our listening ears, she gradually started to open up about the dark side of the history of the place. She spoke about how her people had been told that they couldn't use sweet grass as incense within the church. She told us about the residential school. She showed us the various plaques with their historical inscriptions and she pointed out the beautiful stained glass windows. Then she pointed to the pew on which she, as a little girl, would come to lie down and cry. Then she took us to the narthex, and showed us a cupboard: "This is where they would take the boys and abuse them."

It was my task that day to thank our host at the end of our visit on behalf of the group. Thanks, however, seemed woefully inadequate. I did thank her, for her graciousness and for showing us her beautiful chapel. Then I apologized. "As a Canadian, and as an Anglican, I am so sorry for what we did to you and your people."

On June 11, 2008, Prime Minister Steven Harper apologized to former students of residential schools on behalf of the government of Canada, acknowledging the profoundly negative consequences of the schools; the lasting and damaging impact on Aboriginal culture, heritage and language; the abuse and neglect of helpless children; and the legacy of residential schools and their role in contributing to social problems that continue to exist in many communities today.

The Truth and Reconciliation Commission was established in part "to guide and inspire a process of truth and healing, leading towards reconciliation within Aboriginal families, and between Aboriginal and non-Aboriginal communities, churches, governments, and Canadians generally."

The TRC criss-crossed the country, listening to and documenting the stories told by residential school survivors, of their oppression and abuse. The seventh and final national TRC event to hear first-hand the witness and experience of those who attended residential schools took place in Edmonton in late March of 2014. It may have been the final TRC event, but it was just the beginning of what will be a long and difficult journey towards reconciliation.

The reading on which I based my sermon for that Sunday was from the Gospel of John.

As he walked along, he saw a man blind from birth. His disciples asked him, "Rabbi, who sinned, this man or his parents, that he was born blind?" Jesus answered, "Neither this man nor his parents sinned; he was born blind so that God's works might be revealed in him. We must work the works of him who sent me while it is day; night is coming when no one can work. As long as I am in the world, I am the light of the world." When he had said this, he spat on the ground and made mud with the saliva and spread the mud on the man's eyes, saying to him, "Go, wash in the pool of Siloam" (which means Sent). Then he went and washed and came back able to see...

They brought to the Pharisees the man who had formerly been blind. Now it was a Sabbath day when Jesus made the mud and opened his eyes. Then the Pharisees also began to ask him how he had received his sight. He said to them, "He put mud on my eyes. Then I washed, and now I see." Some of the Pharisees said, "This man is not from God, for he does not observe the Sabbath." But others said, "How can a man who is a sinner perform such signs?" And they were divided. So they said again to the blind man, "What do you say about him? It was your eyes he opened." He said, "He is a prophet."...

Then they reviled him, saying, "You are his disciple, but we are disciples of Moses. We know that God has spoken to Moses, but as for this man, we do not know where he comes from"... And they drove him out.

Jesus heard that they had driven him out, and when he found him, he said, "Do you believe in the Son of Man?" He answered, "And who is he, sir? Tell me, so that I may believe in him." Jesus said to him, "You have seen him, and the one speaking with you is he." He said, "Lord, I believe." And he worshipped him. Jesus said, "I came into this world for judgment so that those who do not see may see, and those who do see may become blind." Some of the Pharisees near him heard this and said to him, "Surely we are not blind, are we?" (John 9:1–7, 13–17, 28–29, 34b–40, NRSV).

SERMON

"Surely We're Not Blind, Are We?"[5]

This week, the federal government released a report called "Invisible Women: A Call to Action. A report on missing and murdered Indigenous women in Canada." In this document, it was reported that Indigenous women and girls are three times more likely to be the target of violent victimization than non-Indigenous woman and girls, and that the number of known cases of missing or murdered Indigenous women and girls in Canada is 668[6]. The report highlights "the silence that is part of the ongoing trend of main-stream society with respect to Aboriginal people," which has rendered these women "invisible."

Surely we're not blind, are we?

This week, thousands of people, including Archbishop Fred Hiltz, the Primate of the Anglican Church of Canada, are gathered in Edmonton for the final national Truth and Reconciliation Commission event. The TRC was established in 2008 in the wake of the Canadian government apology to Indigenous peoples on behalf of all Canadians for the Indian residential schools system. The residential schools system operated in Canada for over a century, beginning in the 1870s. The two principle objectives of the residential schools system were to remove and isolate children from the influence of their homes, families, traditions and cultures, and to assimilate them into the dominant culture.

Surely we're not blind, are we?

This week in our gospel reading, Jesus heals a man born blind. When the man who was blind but who now sees refuses to criticize Jesus for breaking the Sabbath law, the leaders of the community condemn him for being born entirely in sin and drive him out of the community. Then they say to Jesus, "Surely we're not blind, are we?"

In John's gospel, Jesus is the light that shines in the darkness, the light that has come into the world, the light that enlightens all people. This is not in doubt. What *is* in doubt is our response. When we see the light, do we turn towards it, or do we turn away and persist in our blindness?

John uses the story of the healing of a blind man as a dramatic parable of what happens when light comes into the world. Jesus is the light that has come into the world, full of grace and truth. But as we see in today's gospel, the encounter with Jesus is a disorienting grace and an inconvenient truth.

Grace is revealed in the healing of a man who was blind from birth. His healing is a gift of God, an act of goodness. You would expect the response to be joy, thanksgiving, and wonder. But apart from the man himself, no one in this drama seems to be happy about it. There is no cry of "how wonderful" or "thank God!" Rather, the response to grace is confusion, division, and suspicion. I've often thought that the confused responses and interrogations would make a good Monty Python skit, that is, until I get to the part where the parents are so fearful that they can't even celebrate the provision of sight to their son, and then the part where the man who was formerly blind is driven out of the community by the angry leaders.

Truth is revealed when Jesus gives sight to the blind man. This healing is a sign that Jesus is from God. Sometimes it takes a while for the truth to sink in. The man who is given his sight at first refers to Jesus as "the man called Jesus," then a bit later as "a prophet," then in the second interrogation as a "man from God," and finally he acknowledges Jesus as the "Son of Man," and worships him. His is a journey of recognition; of learning to see.

The response of the Pharisees is very different. For them, the truth signified by the healing is inconvenient, because it involves a violation of the Sabbath law. To truly see what this healing signifies, they would have to let go of their understanding of the law. They would have to let go of their understanding of what it means to be a disciple of Moses. That would be hard. These understandings provide comfort and meaning and coherence to their lives, and guarantee their positions of power and privilege.

Faced with a truth that is too inconvenient, too painful, their reaction is both tragic and predictable. First, they try to deny that the healing ever happened. When that doesn't work, when it is clearly established that this man who can see is indeed the man who was blind from birth, they take aim at the man himself. The bearer of the inconvenient truth is discredited, demonized, and expelled from the community. The grace was too disorienting. The light that comes into the world is too painful to look at.

This story is, after all, not so much a story of the blindness of the man whose sight is restored. It's much more a story about the blindness of those around him, of the Pharisees who are not able to see what is really going on.

But it's also *our* story. Like the Pharisees, we have a great need for security, comfort, and certainty. We need to make sense of things. We need to impose order on a world that sometimes seems chaotic. We need to make meaning out of events that sometimes seem random. We need to feel we have control of our lives. In order to meet all these very human needs, we and our communities and our culture wrap ourselves in strand after strand of understandings and assumptions and rules and conventions and philosophies and conveniences until, strand by strand, we have wrapped ourselves into a cocoon. We think that we see very well in that cocoon, but really we're blind to the greater reality that lies beyond the silk walls that surround us.

Then, just when we feel safe and secure, something or someone comes along and rattles our world. It might be that moment your spouse tells you she is thinking of leaving, when you thought that you had a good marriage. It might be the call from the school telling you that your kid is doing drugs, when you thought you had everything under control as good parents. It might be that first allegation of abuse within the residential school system we thought we had set up for the benefit of Indigenous children. It might be the scientific evidence that the economic system we thought would lead us to prosperity is actually destroying the planet. It might be the dawning realization of a man such as John Newton, the captain of a slave-trading ship in the 18th century, that the slave trade is an abomination.

How often are we comfortably wrapped up in our cocoon when, all of a sudden, someone pokes a hole in our covering and lets light shine into our darkness. It's disorienting. The light hurts our eyes. At first we may feel that we can't see anymore because of the glare, and we may react by attacking the one who poked the hole in our cocoon. We try to patch the hole as quickly as we can.

How do we respond to disorienting grace, to inconvenient truth, to light that reveals the darkness?

The message of this gospel is that the most dangerous thing, spiritually speaking, is to live in the delusion that we can see – that we are fully-sighted. We want to think that we can see. We need to make sense of the world, to impose order on the chaos we experience, to feel that we have a grasp on things, and that we are in control.

The problem for us as spiritual beings is that we are called to be in relationship with others and with the one we call God. And, when we are in relationship, we are *never* completely in control. Our way of seeing can never be the last word.

Especially when we're in relationship with God, who is ultimately a mystery to us. To be in relationship with God is to live in a constant state of disequilibrium, to be a pilgrim on a journey, not someone who has arrived at a destination. We don't have everything figured out. If we think we do, we're blind.

But if we can acknowledge our condition as journeyers, as people who are *not* fully-sighted, as seekers, not possessors of the truth, then we can journey towards the light knowing that it can enlighten our path and provide guidance on our way. When we encounter Jesus, when we encounter disorienting grace in our lives, we can receive it as a gift, even if that means we need to let go of other things to free up our hands. When we encounter inconvenient truth, we can re-joice in the truth, even if that truth is cause for lament as well.

It took John Newton the slave trader five years after he first encountered Christ to give up the slave trade, and another 20 before he started to campaign against it. He wrote of his encounter with grace in the hymn we know well.

Amazing grace, how sweet the sound, that saved a wretch like me. I once was lost, but now am found, was blind but now I see.

It took John Newton 30 years to write that hymn. It has taken Canadian churches and Canadian society an even longer time to journey out of the blindness of the residential school system that we imposed on Indigenous peoples in Canada. Today is the final event of a process that was launched six years ago with the hope of healing the wounds and the blindness that are the consequence and cause of the residential schools system. People will tell their stories. It will be a time of inconvenient truth and disorienting grace. It is just the beginning.

Jesus says, "I am the light of the world." The light has come into the world, full of disorienting grace and inconvenient truth. May those of us who are blind turn towards that light and learn to see.

1. *Honouring the Truth, Reconciling for the Future: Summary of the Final Report of the Truth and Reconciliation Commission of Canada*, July 23, 2015, http://www.trc.ca/websites/trcinstitution/File/2015/ Honouring_the_Truth_Reconciling_for_the_Future_July_23_2015.pdf (accessed March 4, 2017), v.
2. *Honouring the Truth*, 2.
3. *Honouring the Truth*, 3.
4. "Apology to Native People: A Message from the Primate, Archbishop Michael Peers, to the National Native Convocation Minaki, Ontario, Friday, August 6, 1993," The Anglican Church of Canada, http:// www.anglican.ca/wp-content/uploads/2011/06/Apology-English.pdf (accessed March 4, 2017).

5. Sermon: Lent 4 –March 30, 2014. Readings: 1 Samuel 16:1–13; Psalm 23; Ephesians 5:8–14; John 9:1–41.
6. Subsequent reports have assessed the number of missing and murdered Indigenous women and girls in Canada to be much higher. See for example the 2014 RCMP report *Missing and Murdered Aboriginal Women: A National Operational Overview,* http://www.rcmp-grc.gc.ca/en/missing-and-murdered-aboriginal-women-national-operational-overview#sec1 (accessed July 17, 2017).

SIX

Evolution

The publication of **Charles Darwin's** *On the Origin of Species* in 1859 was the key event in an intellectual revolution that posed a three-fold challenge to Christian thought in the 19th century. First, evolutionary theory challenged what was called the argument from design, the classic 19th century justification for the existence of God based on the perceived design inherent in nature and articulated by people like William Paley. Second, evolution challenged prevailing ideas of human dignity and distinctiveness by treating humanity as an integral part of nature, with no sharp dividing line separating human and animal life. Third, evolutionary theory challenged the assumption that the characteristics of all living things were fixed when they were created.

Cast more broadly, this was a challenge to biblical literalism, and to the literal interpretation of the seven-day creation story in Genesis in particular. This is not to say that all Christians interpreted Genesis literally. As far back as St. Augustine in the fourth century, symbolic interpretations of Genesis had been proposed by Christian theologians. But in the second half of the 19th century, in the midst of an ongoing debate about biblical interpretation, the three-fold challenge of evolutionary theory was a major disruption, and one that helped to create divisions that persist today.

Over the intervening years, most Christians have made peace

with the theory of evolution in its modern form, despite a vocal minority who still reject Darwin and his successors. But even for the majority of Christians who have accepted evolution, the level of engagement with the science is not all that high. We accept that evolution and a traditional Christian understanding of God are compatible, that the creation stories in Genesis can be understood metaphorically and symbolically, and we may say things like "if God wanted to create the universe by an evolutionary process, well, so be it!"

But an opportunity exists to go beyond simple acceptance. How does evolution impact our understanding of God? of ourselves? of divine action? How does it inform the way we imagine God? If, as St. Paul writes in Romans 1:20, "ever since the creation of the world, God's eternal power and divine nature, invisible though they are, have been understood and seen through the things God has made," then what new things can we understand and see about God in this new story of creation?

That sort of exploration appealed to the scientist in me. So when the Vatican announced a conference on evolution, I decided to attend. The year 2009 was both the 200th anniversary of the birth of Charles Darwin and the 150th anniversary of the publication of *On the Origin of Species*. In honour of these anniversaries, the Vatican organized an international conference – *Biological Evolution: Facts and Theories* – as an opportunity for scientists, philosophers, and theologians to reconsider biological evolution, its recent developments and the ideological debate that often accompanies it in theological circles.

The conference featured an impressive lineup of speakers organized by the Pontifical Gregorian University and the University of Notre Dame. It started with the science – the evidence as we know it – and then progressed to the topic of evolutionary mechanisms. Next up was anthropology, including the question of human origins. Finally, the conference addressed the philosophical and theological aspects of evolution. It was a remarkable and unusual gathering, with brilliant scientists, philosophers, and theologians all together in the same room.

On the second last day of the conference, one of the presenters, a philosopher of science, managed to put my developing thoughts into words: "the evolutionary world view should be received as an urge to renovate theological thinking." That made sense to me on a personal level. In the 1980s, quantum physics had provided the opportunity to renovate my theological thinking. Now it was the turn of biology.

While I was at the conference immersing myself in biological evolution, I also had a look at the psalm which would be read the coming Sunday. It was one of my favourites, Psalm 19, and that week it had a particular significance.

The heavens declare the glory of God, and the firmament shows the handiwork of the Lord.
One day tells its tale to another, and one night imparts knowledge to another.
Although they have no words or language, and their voices are not heard,
their sound has gone out into all lands, and their message to the ends of the world.
In the deep has God set a pavilion for the sun; it comes forth like a bridegroom out of his chamber;
it rejoices like a champion to run its course.
It goes forth from the uttermost edge of the heavens and runs about to the end of it again;
nothing is hidden from its burning heat (Psalm 19:1–6, *Trial Use Liturgical Psalter*, 2016, The Anglican Church of Canada).

One of the ironies of history is that this beautiful song, which urges us to discover the glory of God in the beauty and workings of creation, was actually one of the texts used in the 16th century to oppose the Copernican Revolution. Copernicus, in his work *On the Revolutions of the Heavenly Spheres*, had proposed that the earth moves around the sun, contradicting the prevailing view of the earth as fixed at the centre of the universe. "Nonsense," said some of the theologians. "Psalm 19 tells us that it is the sun that moves, 'running its course from the uttermost edge of the heavens to the end of it again each day.'" Oops!

What Psalm 19 *really* proclaims in poetic language is how the universe reflects God's glory. It celebrates the way in which creation, the sun, the stars – and for me that week, the natural history of evolution – act as a portal that lets us see and know the things of God, "God's eternal power and divine nature," to use the words of St. Paul. Because when you allow creation to tell its story – a story that begins with the mystery of the Big Bang and continues with the crazy expansion of the universe; the creation of those vast engines of nuclear fission called stars, which generate the heavy elements needed for life; the cooling of the galaxies; the formation of our planet Earth, with its waters and atmosphere; the molecular relationships that created organic building blocks; the emergence of life itself; the evolutionary story of the generation and diversification of life forms and eventually of species; the birth of humanity with its consciousness and cultures – this is an epic story, and it rightly fires our imagination about the God who is creator of all.

The evolutionary story offers us a dynamic picture of reality, one in which change and becoming are woven into the fabric of the universe, and of ourselves. As the 20th-century theologian Karl Rahner puts it, the human is a created being in the process of becoming. Evolutionary science also shines a light on the pivotal role of relationships at every level: physical, chemical, biological, symbiotic, and cultural. There is a wonderful interplay between order and randomness: the universe as we know it could not have come into being without the order that we usually identify as natural laws, and yet, it is randomness that produced the variations and differences in life forms that made the evolution of life possible. When we look at the story of the universe, we discover that we are here despite the odds, and that the natural laws that provided the potential for our becoming turn out to have natural constants that have been fine-tuned for the possibility of our existence. This is often called the anthropic principle, and for many it suggests the likelihood that God was involved.

Of all the known universe, our planet in particular seems to have an impulse towards life – abundant life that emerges in and adapts to a huge diversity of environments and eco-systems, life that seems to revel in immense variety. There is an evident beauty in nature, one that we as creatures of this universe take delight in. And yet, that natural beauty has a shadow side. We know that most animals on this planet die a painful death. That is the cost of a dynamic universe and an evolving world. The recognition of this shadow side allows the evolutionary understanding to provide a context for theodicy, the theological reflection on the problem of suffering.

Biologists are cautious in assigning purpose or directionality to any of these natural evolutionary processes. But they certainly recognize the phenomenon of emergence, and the impulse towards organization. As life forms evolve, processes and behaviours emerge at higher levels that cannot be reduced to a combination of those expressed at lower levels. Preeminent, at least for us, among these emergent processes is human consciousness. One of the paleontologists at the conference offered that, from what he had learned about natural history, it seems highly likely from the outset that consciousness would emerge. Both a directional and a theistic reading of the evolutionary story are well within reach, though by no means a given. When we allow ourselves to be immersed in the epic story of cosmology and natural history, we do indeed have the opportunity to hear the message that the stars and the lifeforms of our universe are proclaiming about the glory of God, and to do a little reimagining.

SERMON

ReImagining God[1]

When is the last time that you reimagined God? We all conjure up various images, pictures, and names whenever the word "God" is mentioned. Most of us have a default mode that we go to when we imagine God. Perhaps it's the old man with the long white beard sitting on a throne and acting as judge. Perhaps it's the mysterious force that we hear about in the *Star Wars* movies. But whatever your image or images, when is the last time you set them aside and tried to reimagine God?

In Psalm 19, the poet imagines God as both Creator, the great artist of nature, and as the Giver of the Law, the one who gave the Torah to the people of Israel. For good measure, the poet also throws in images of God as rock and as redeemer. The scriptures are full of many different images for God, acknowledging that none of our images can fully capture what and who God is. When St. Augustine, the great bishop and theologian of the fourth century, was asked what God is, he replied "God is mystery." It was his way of saying that none of our names for God, nor our images for God, can contain all that God is. God is, if you like, too big for our words and pictures.

I think that is why it's good that we have so many images and names for God – a multiplicity of metaphors that can at times contradict each other and at other times open up new inspiration for our imaginations. Paul Ricoeur, the French theologian, called this a "polyphonic naming of God," and he thought it was a good thing.

But out of this multiplicity of images, we often tend to get stuck on one. Maybe it's God the omnipotent being. Maybe it's God the king, sitting on his throne. But whatever it is, sometimes we can focus on this one *image* and mistake it for God. We can wrap all sorts of theology around our chosen image, and years of tradition and history, until the image grows so strong that it becomes very difficult to give it up. It takes on a life of its own. Our image becomes an idol.

We are warned about the dangers of idolatry in our first reading from the book of Exodus, the Ten Commandments. Near the top of the list, God tells the people of Israel, "You shall not make for yourself an idol, whether in the form of anything that is in heaven above, or on earth beneath, or in the water under the earth. You shall not bow down or worship them."

Idols take many forms in our modern world. The love of money, self-centredness, pleasure-seeking, materialism – these are all idols we worship today. But it is also idolatry when we think we have God all figured out, if we think we have God by the tail. When we get stuck on any one image of God and build our religious practices around that image, we run the risk of idolatry. Which is why it is good for our spiritual health to reimagine God from time to time, and to allow ourselves to consider new pictures and names for who God is.

Dealing with a new image of God can be a difficult thing, however. Paul writes about that in the second reading that we heard this morning: his letter to the Corinthians. In Jesus, we have been given a radically new and disturbing image for God – the God who, in Jesus, hung on the cross and was crucified. It is an image of humiliation, of suffering, of vulnerability, of weakness. This is the message about the cross that Paul proclaimed, the image of Christ crucified. And people were disturbed by it. To the Jews, who were expecting God to send a triumphant messiah to defeat their Roman oppressors, this image of a messiah crucified by those same Romans was a stumbling block. To the Gentiles, whose image of God was inspired by Greek philosophy, the idea of a crucified God was foolish. God was the supreme being, omnipotent, omniscient, impassible and all those other fancy words the Greek philosophers used to describe God. The God of Greek philosophy couldn't possibly suffer at the hands of human beings. The image of God as Christ crucified was utter foolishness. And yet, that is what Paul proclaimed.

In our gospel reading today, we have the account of Jesus clearing the animals and money-changers out of the temple. This, too, is an instance when people were forced to reimagine God. The Jewish authorities thought that they had things figured out. Yahweh was the lawgiver, whose presence on earth was in the temple in Jerusalem. When people broke the laws that Yahweh had given, they had to come to the temple to offer sacrifice in order to atone for their sins. A well-defined religious system had been built around this image of God. And yet, it had gone wrong. Religion had become a business, the temple a marketplace. An oppressive system had been put in place that forced the poor to pay money that ended up in the pockets of the rich. In the gospel, Jesus takes a public stand against the use of religion to oppress people; it was a demonstration against the materialism that had become part of temple worship. If this is what you think God is all about, then it's time to rethink your image of God. God's presence is not to be found in the temple, but rather in the actions and person of Jesus.

It is spiritually healthy for *all* of us to reimagine God from time to time. I recently had the opportunity to do just that. Last week I was in Rome attending a conference on evolution organized by the Vatican in honour of the 150th anniversary of Darwin's *On the Origin of Species*. Some Christians are disturbed by the theory of evolution. The account that evolution provides of how living things on earth came to be conflicts with their understanding of how God created the world.

One of the dominant images of God the creator in our tradition is that of an omnipotent father-like figure who lives in heaven. According to this image, God reached down into our world and crafted the various plants and animals at the beginning, but from then on only intervenes from time to time in our affairs as necessary.

Immersing myself in the story of evolution for a week provided an opportunity to loosen that image of God and to do some re-imagining. If we take seriously the idea that the world was created through the processes of evolution, what image of God can emerge?

First of all, nature itself reveals certain things to us. It reveals that the world is in continuous creation, that new species emerge as others disappear. Creation is not static, but rather dynamic.

Nature also reveals that there is an impulse towards life on this earth. Life is found in the most unlikely places: in the driest, coldest deserts of Antarctica and in the superheated water of undersea volcanic vents. The direction of creation, at least on this planet, is towards abundance of life. And not just abundance, but variety. The variety found in the millions of species that have lived on the earth is stunning. There is, however, a shadow side to this dynamism and variety; the same combination of order and chance that produces the variety of life also results in the disappearance of life forms. Suffering, at least in this sense, seems to be an intrinsic aspect of a dynamic creation.

Another surprise that awaits us as we study evolution is the importance of relationships. Whether we're talking about the molecular relationships created by finely balanced electrochemical attractions, or the symbiotic relationships created by different life forms living in close contact, relationships have emerged as central to our understanding of how life evolves. All of the major transitions of evolutionary theory – the origin of life, the first nucleated cell, the emergence of humans – all of these transitions have happened because of relationships, either through symbiogenesis or the emergence of behaviours that benefit the group rather than the individual.

And so what image of God emerges from all this? It is an image of a God who loves life in all its abundance, who loves variety; and for whom relationships are central. It is an image in which God is a dynamic presence rather than an unchanging and distant being. This God does not act by overwhelming power and control, but rather from within, as a subtle presence within creation; inspiring, sustaining, nudging things along. This God favours relationships, and suffers with all creatures.

You may recognize this image of God. In our Christian tradition, it sounds a lot like God the Holy Spirit, the oft-neglected person in our Trinitarian understanding of God. We tend to focus on God the Father and God the Son, but maybe we should allow ourselves to spend time with God the Spirit.

My recent trip gave me the opportunity to do some re-imagining of God. May you have the opportunity to do the same.

1. Sermon: Lent 3 – March 15, 2009. Readings: Exodus 20:1–17; Psalm 19; 1 Corinthians 1:18–25; John 2:13–22.

SEVEN

Why Bad Things Happen

Bad stuff happens. Not one week passes that something bad doesn't happen to someone I know. Sometimes it's bad in an unpleasant way. Sometimes it's bad in a tragic or fatal way. When we extend our gaze to include what we see on the news, pain and suffering become a daily or hourly occurrence, their frequency limited only by how often we are willing to look. As preachers, as pastors, it's something we need to talk about. And yet we know the challenges. The question of theodicy, of why there is pain and suffering in the world that God created, is an ancient question. For millennia, we have tendered varied, contradictory, and incomplete responses. For some, the problem of suffering is an intellectual roadblock to faith, an argument against the existence of God. For others, it's personal, existential, a present reality. Either way, a response is called for, but timing matters; to talk theology in response to the anguish of another person can be irrelevant, insensitive, or worse.

Sometimes a story allows us to slide into a space sideways when a frontal assault would simply rally our defences. In our scriptures, the story that wrestles with the problem of pain is the Book of Job. Once upon a time, in the land of Uz, there lived a man whose name was Job. It is an ancient Hebrew story, set down in writing over 2,000 years ago, mostly in poetic form. The protagonist, Job, is a good person, a leading citizen, a wealthy man who through no fault of his own loses everything – his wealth, his health, his children. The question has been posed. What will be the response?

Then Job answered:
"Today also my complaint is bitter;
his hand is heavy despite my groaning.
O that I knew where I might find God,
that I might come even to the Lord's dwelling!
I would lay my case before God,
and fill my mouth with arguments.
I would learn what God would answer me,
and understand what the Lord would say to me.
Would God contend with me in the greatness of God's power?
No; but God would give heed to me...

Then the Lord answered Job out of the whirlwind (Job 23:1–6, 38:1, *NRSV* adapted).

SERMON

Why Bad Things Happen[1]

The book of Job is one of the most challenging, profound and, I dare say, relevant books of the Bible, and so I want to spend some time talking about it, though we will only scratch the surface.

I expect many of us are at least somewhat familiar with the story. Once upon a time in a land far away, there was a man named Job, a very prosperous man with wealth and servants and many children. Now Job was a blameless and upright man who feared God. Even God holds Job up as an example of righteousness. But Satan – not the devil, but an associate of God in God's holy court – suggests to God that the only reason Job is so good and so religious is that he has been rewarded for it and is prosperous as a result. According to Satan, Job's religion is nothing more than enlightened self-interest. God disagrees and allows Satan to put Job to the test. And so Job is stripped of everything he has. His livestock are stolen, his servants are murdered, a house collapses and kills his children, and then Job himself is struck with painful and loathsome sores from the soles of his feet to the crown of his head. Eventually, we find Job in misery, sitting in a heap of ashes, scraping his skin with a shard of pottery.

This initial prologue is intended to set up the main part of the story, which follows. But first, a couple of comments. We know from the language that this is a fable or a parable, and what we've heard so far is intended to set up what is to come. In other words, we don't need to worry too much about the disturbing picture of God that we find in this introduction to the story, a God who is willing to ruin someone's life in order to settle a dispute amongst the heavenly beings. That's just the setup needed to get us to Job on the ash heap. What we *do* need to know in order to continue with the story is that, first, Job is truly innocent, and second, the suffering that has come upon him is, from Job's perspective, extreme, undeserved, and in-explicable.

The prologue also sets up the first question of the book of Job, and it might not be the one you expect. The first question we encounter is this: Does religion depend on a system of reward and punishment? Or to flip it around, if there was no system of reward and punishment, would humans still be faithful? Is religious behaviour no more than enlightened self-interest? Will Job, faced with his unjust suffering, curse God and die, as his wife suggests he should, or will he maintain his integrity and his faith in God?

We like systems of reward and punishment. Who among us has not cried out "that's not fair" at some point in our life? A prominent theology in the Old Testament – the theology embraced by Job himself and by the friends who come to "comfort" him in his distress – is that God rewards the righteous and punishes the wicked. It is a theology of retributive justice, often associated with the book of Deuteronomy. Why do people suffer? According to this theology, suffering is due to sin.

But as Job found out, this theology of retributive justice doesn't always fit the realities of life. Christianity has mostly, but not completely, moved away from the idea of reward and punishment in this life. But systems of reward and punishment persist, especially the notion of reward and punishment in the next life. Heaven and hell, with rules and requirements that determine which way you're going. Baptism as an entry into heaven. Forgiveness as dependent on confession and doing penance. Indulgences as a way of lessening time in purgatory. Or, more recently, the notion that you're only going to get to heaven if you "accept Jesus as your personal saviour."

Why are these systems of reward and punishment so persistent in our tradition? Why are they so attractive to so many of us? One reason might be because they're very satisfying psychologically. They give us order. They give us power and control. If I know the rules and can comply with them, then I have power and control over my own destiny.

But there's also a problem with this. Operating within a system of reward and punishment can lead to self-interest rather than authentic relationship. Do I truly love God with all my heart, soul, mind, and strength? Or is my faith nothing more than enlightened self-interest operating within a framework of reward and punishment?

Now let's go back to Job on the ash heap. When his world comes crashing down, when he suffers unjustly and his theology of reward and punishment is called into question, what will he do? Will he curse God? No, despite all that has happened, Job maintains his faith in God. The book of Job's answer to our first question is yes, there can be faith beyond reward and punishment. Yes, there is the possibility of authentic relationship with God.

But that's not the question you're most interested in, is it? The question that grabs most of us is the second question of the book of Job: Why do bad things happen to good people? Why do bad things happen at all, to anyone? What do we do, what do we say about God in the midst of extreme, undeserved, and unexplained suffering?

As Job sits on the ash heap, scraping his sores, three friends come to visit. And one by one, they start to explain what has happened to Job. They all operate out of the world view of retributive justice, that the righteous are rewarded and the wicked are punished. They tell Job that he must be responsible for his own downfall. They tell Job that he must have sinned and that he should examine himself and repent of his sin. When Job insists that he is innocent and that God is treating him unfairly, his "friends" defend God. In fact, the more Job protests his innocence, the more his friends find their own orderly world view threatened, and the more vicious their attacks on Job become. "Is not your wickedness great" his so-called friends tell him, in a desperate attempt to keep their own theology from falling into chaos.

Needless to say, Job's friends are not very helpful, so Job turns from talking about God with his companions to talking directly to God. We call this prayer. More specifically, we call this lament – the prayer of those who suffer, the prayer of those who scream out to God in anger, grief, pain, and despair. It is as if Job is clinging to God with one hand and shaking his fist at him with the other. He holds on to God with a fierce faith, but refuses to let God off the hook for the inexplicable suffering that shadows our world.

And we learn something here: the better response to suffering is not theology, but prayer. In the face of suffering, it is better to talk *to* God, than to talk *about* God. Maybe that's the reason for the first question of the book of Job, and the response which asserts that yes, there is the possibility of authentic relationship with God. Our response to the question of suffering will be built on that relationship. As Job laments, as he pours out his heart to God, there is movement. Job's words change from expressing his desire to die, to crying out for justice. He wants to find God, to lay his case before him, to prove to God that he is innocent.

And suddenly God answers Job out of the whirlwind.

Who is this that darkens counsel by words without knowledge?
Gird up your loins like a man,
I will question you, and you shall declare to me.
Where were you when I laid the foundation of the earth?
Tell me if you have understanding.
Who determined its measurements – surely you know? ...
    who shut in the sea with doors when it burst out from the womb?
    ... Who has cut a channel for the torrents of rain,
and a way for the thunderbolt,
to bring rain on a land where no one lives ...
and to make the ground put forth grass?

Is it by your wisdom that the hawk soars
and spreads its wings toward the south?

Can you draw out Leviathan with a fish hook
or press down its tongue with a cord? ...

From its mouth go flaming torches;
sparks of fire leap out (Job 38:2–5a, 8, 25–26, 27b; 39:26; 41:1, 19,
NRSV).

God's response to Job extends through four chapters of the book. It
is fascinating to me as a quantum physicist that there are two long
sections in this poem dedicated to Behemoth and Leviathan, the two
mythical monsters of ancient times that represent chaos and
randomness. In recent times, scientists have rediscovered just how
important chaos and randomness actually are. When you dig down
deep to the subatomic level, there are no discernable causes for
individual events. Stuff happens randomly.

Now, there are overall patterns and probabilities that make our
lives predictable in many ways. When I drop a pen, I can be confident
that it will fall to the floor. But microscopic events – such as the
genetic mutations that enabled the evolution of human beings but
that also generate cancer cells – these are random processes. For
some reason that only God knows, God has created a world, a
universe, that is majestic and beautiful, but also dynamic in a way
that allows for chaos and randomness within the limits set by God,
enabling creation itself to be wild and free. This is the world that
God made and that God loves, a world that is beautiful and good and
free and wild and grace-filled, a world that is much bigger than
ourselves, a world that is not entirely safe for human beings, a world
where good stuff happens and bad stuff happens to good people and
bad people alike.

When God speaks out of the whirlwind, he does not answer Job's
questions. Instead, he paints a picture and invites Job to live in this
world. Job's response is awe and wonder, and he places his hand
over his mouth.

Out of the whirlwind, God breaks Job's world wide-open. You
see, Job used to feel that he was at the centre of the universe:
prosperous, important, people sought him out, all of that stuff. But
God shows him that creation is not centred on Job. It's not even
centred on human beings. It's much, much bigger!

Job used to think he had everything figured out, that he knew the rules: the righteous would be rewarded, the wicked would be punished, and if he could just play by the rules, he would remain in control of his own life. But God shows him that the world is much wilder than that, and that it is not nearly as safe and predictable as Job used to think.

But God shows Job one more thing as well. Even though Job is not as important as he thought he was and even though his life is not as safe and as predictable as he thought it was and even though Job realizes that he comprehends much less than he thought he did, God offers Job something much more valuable – the possibility of living in authentic relationship with God.

Before, says Job, "I had heard about you" but now he says, "my eye sees you."

And here, the transformation of Job is complete. He still sits on the ash heap; he still has his sores, he still suffers. But he has moved, first from wanting to die, then to crying out for justice, then, to being overwhelmed by awe and wonder, and finally, to the determination to live again. He will live in this wild and beautiful world that God has created and he will do so in relationship with God. Job's life may be a whirlwind, a whirlwind of suffering and uncertainty and injustice. But even in the whirlwind, God speaks and God is with us.[2]

1. Sermon: October 25, 2015. Readings: Selections from the book of Job.
2. Those who have read the whole of the book of Job will know that a prosaic ending has been added to the main poetic body of the text in which Job gains a new family and regains his material wealth. It is the sort of ending that many readers, and certainly advocates of retributive justice, would want. Rather than discuss this at length here, I simply invite readers to do a little self-examination and to ponder the question, "Do you need this 'happy ending' in order to say that Job's story ended well?"

EIGHT

A Brutal Year

Summers are supposed to be a lighter time of year. Commitments ease, vacations kick in, the weather is warm, and there is a certain lightness of being when compared with the other seasons. At least, that's what we hope for. But the summer of 2014 carried with it a distinct heaviness. I could feel it in our community. A congruence of bad news from around the world was weighing on us, bringing us down. That's unusual. Typically we manage to keep a safe distance from the events that unfold on our screens and in our newspapers. It's not often that distant events conspire to pierce and overwhelm our psychological defences.

Perhaps a starting point for our summer malaise could be located at the beginning of the new year, with the capture of the town of Fallujah in Northern Iraq. The victors subsequently proclaimed themselves as the Islamic State, also known by its initials, ISIS (the Islamic State of Iraq and Syria). Sadly, war in Iraq is nothing new. Neither is the tragic civil war in Syria, which has been raging since 2011, displacing millions and killing hundreds of thousands. But it was the beheadings that shook us. In July, ISIS beheaded 75 captured Syrian soldiers, recording the executions on video and sharing them around the world via social media for maximum effect. This was followed a month later by the beheading of James Foley, an American journalist. We were outraged and disgusted by these displays of brutality. There was an incongruence in the marriage of a barbarism we associate with ancient times and the social media of our modern era.

At the time, we were still recovering from the news that four boys playing on a beach in Gaza had been killed by Israeli naval fire. Israel had launched a military operation in Gaza in July with the stated aim of stopping rocket fire from Gaza into Israel. The true cost of that military operation struck home with the death of those four boys, a "tragic mistake" in the words of the subsequent Israeli investigation. But it wasn't just the wars, though that would have been enough. That same July, we found out that the Ebola epidemic that had been identified in Guinea in March had now spread to Liberia, Sierra Leone and Nigeria, and the number of new cases and deaths was increasing exponentially. By the first week in August, the death toll had reached one thousand; four weeks later, it had more than doubled.

Then, there was Ferguson. On August 9, an 18-year-old African-American man, Michael Brown, was fatally shot by a white male police officer in Ferguson, Missouri. Brown's death followed on the heels of the death in New York City of Eric Garner, another young African American who died after a police officer put him in a chokehold while arresting him. Ferguson became the ignition point for an explosion of anger at the ongoing problem of racism within the police and the criminal justice system in America. The streets of Ferguson filled with protestors and some in the crowds began looting. Police responded with curfews and riot squads, tear gas and rubber bullets. A state of emergency was declared by the Missouri state governor. The National Guard was called in. More than 600 people were arrested. Protestors walked through Ferguson with their hands in the air shouting "Don't Shoot." The hashtag #BlackLivesMatter went viral on social media as an entire nation confronted once more the problem of racism in its midst.

Those of us in other places lived at a safe physical distance from all of this. And yet, psychologically and spiritually, we were failing to keep our distance. There is value to be sure in feeling empathy for those who suffer, in lowering our defensive walls on occasion. We know that we are the fortunate ones, insulated by history and geography from the tragedies unfolding around us. But widespread news coverage, social media posts, and exposure to images and video made these events feel close, and the frequency was unrelenting. Perhaps we suffered a form of survivors' guilt, watching the pain of others from the comfort of our living rooms. Whatever the reason, it was getting us down. I could feel it in myself; I could sense it in the voices of others; and I could hear it in the words and the tone as we prayed on Sundays.

In Christian communities, times like these raise both existential and faith questions. Influenced by our culture at large, we still harbour vestiges of the Enlightenment assumption of progress, an assumption which was severely tested in the summer of 2014. We wonder how it is that human beings can do such things to one another. We despair at the apparent intractability of war and conflict. We feel helpless. But, as people of faith, we also ask ourselves how long it will take for God to act. We ask, with the ancient prophet Isaiah, "when will you tear open the heavens and come down?" We don't like to talk about evil, but there are times when we are forced to acknowledge its existence. And we wonder what God will do about it, and when.

In late August, I was invited to attend a three-day preaching workshop which married theatrical skills and drills with the practice of preaching. It was a fresh approach. In addition to working on voice and breathing, posture and presence, we were encouraged to really inhabit the text on which we were working. We were asked to find the point of pain or joy, the place that really moved each one of us and to experience and dwell in that emotion. The text that I was working on was the gospel for the first Sunday in September, from Matthew 18.

If another member of the church sins against you, go and point out the fault when the two of you are alone. If the member listens to you, you have regained that one. But if you are not listened to, take one or two others along with you, so that every word may be confirmed by the evidence of two or three witnesses. If the member refuses to listen to them, tell it to the church; and if the offender refuses to listen even to the church, let such a one be to you as a Gentile and a tax-collector. Truly I tell you, whatever you bind on earth will be bound in heaven, and whatever you loose on earth will be loosed in heaven. Again, truly I tell you, if two of you agree on earth about anything you ask, it will be done for you by my Father in heaven. For where two or three are gathered in my name, I am there among them (Matthew 18:15–20, NRSV).

It was, at first glance, a teaching on church discipline. But in that brutal summer of despair, the words that jumped out at me had nothing to do with church discipline. What struck me, rather, was the apparent promise that "if two of you agree on earth about anything you ask, it will be done for you by my Father in heaven." I really wished it were true. But as the summer of 2014 drew to a close, I wasn't so sure.

SERMON

A Brutal Year[1]

I really wish it were true. I really wish that you and I could come together and share our deepest concerns, and agree on something – anything – to ask, and that it would be done for us by God. I'm thinking of the big asks. I'm thinking about my friend who's being treated for cancer. I'm thinking about the conflicts and suffering in so many places that I've read about in the news lately. I'm thinking about the things that we, as a community, often pray together. I believe that there is power in gathering, and power in coming to agreement. I believe that there is power in asking, and that there is power in prayer. I've seen and experienced that power at work, in my own life and in the lives of others. There are times when I experience prayers as answered. But there are also times when I don't. I really wish it were true that if two people agree on earth about anything they ask, it would be done for them by God. But that's not my experience.

And in that I'm sure I'm not alone. The gospel we read today will be proclaimed by a billion Christians around the world. I wonder how it will be heard. I wonder how it will be heard in northern Iraq, where it will be read in the mountains and in the refugee camps of Christians who have been forced to flee their villages. I wonder how it will be heard in Liberia this morning, by those who sit in quarantine suffering from Ebola. Surely in those places voices have been raised in union this very day asking, pleading with God for healing and for peace, or perhaps simply pleading for enough food and water to survive another night. I pray that it will be done for them. Perhaps it will.

These last months have been brutal. The ongoing civil war in Syria with hundreds of thousands killed and millions displaced from their homes and villages. The Ebola outbreak in West Africa. The war in Gaza, race riots in Ferguson, the beheadings by ISIS, the genocides going on in northern Iraq, the conflict in Ukraine with Russia, not to mention our own personal tragedies, things that never make the headlines but that affect us just as deeply. It's been brutal. What is going on in the world? It is a question many of us are asking. I can't tell you how many people have come up to me during the past month to tell me how angry they are or how saddened they are or how perplexed they are by what's going on. We respond with rage, we respond with depression. And sometimes we wonder, where is God in the midst of all this?

I understand, at least a little, why God can't just do any and everything we ask. Bishop John's article this month in *Crosstalk* is entitled "Where do you put your rage?" When we see a video of a brutal beheading, when we read news reports of children bombed on a beach, we are rightly angry. But just imagine what we might ask for in our rage. We may well respond with words like those in today's psalm, in which the psalmist cries "let a two-edged sword be in their hand, to wreak vengeance on the nations and punishment on the people." Or perhaps we might choose the words of a modern psalmist like Bruce Cockburn: "If I had a rocket launcher... I'd make somebody pay."

And yet, in our rage and in our sadness and in our confusion, in the midst of emotions that so often can isolate us, Jesus calls us to gather together to pray. Justin, the archbishop of Canterbury, put it this way recently: "You can't look at the pictures coming from Gaza and Israel without your heart breaking. We must cry to God and beat down the doors of heaven and pray for peace and justice and security."

When we do, Jesus promises us that God is listening and will respond.

When will God act? How will God respond? I don't know, but I do believe it will be in more ways than we can imagine.

Sometimes we'll be called to be part of that response. I have a friend who found herself moved by the suffering in parts of central Africa – suffering caused by war and conflict, suffering caused by disease and inadequate medical resources. She and many others prayed that those who were suffering there might find healing and peace. Not long afterwards, a flyer from *Médecins Sans Frontières* showed up in her mailbox. Within months, she found herself on a flight to the Central African Republic to work as a nurse practitioner in the MSF clinic there, treating those who were sick and those who had been wounded as a result of the conflict.

But it doesn't always work like that. Sometimes, many times, we can't see anything happening in response to our prayers.

Two weeks ago, I was in Pembroke for a preaching workshop with some other priests of our diocese. While we were there, one of my colleagues received an urgent phone call. She jumped in her car and rushed to a nearby hospital. One of her parishioners was in the intensive care unit, and he and his family had just made the difficult decision to end the blood transfusions that had been keeping him alive but that were no longer working. When my colleague arrived at his side, there was nothing she could do. There wasn't much she could say. And so for the time that she was there she simply sat by his bedside, holding his hand.

Sometimes I think that we focus so much on what needs to be done that we miss the most important part of the promise that Jesus makes in today's gospel: "For where two or three are gathered in my name, I am there among them."

It is the promise of presence. The promise of a God who chose to come into this world to be present as a human being, Emmanuel, God with us. The promise of a God who raised Jesus from the dead so that he might be with us always, to the end of time. The promise of a God who sends his Spirit to be our advocate. There is power in presence, a power we too often miss or dismiss in our habitual rushing around to get things done.

Whenever and wherever people gather in Jesus' name, he is in their midst comforting, encouraging, holding our hands. Today, once again as he promised, Jesus is in the midst of God's people: on the mountains of northern Iraq, in the Ebola wards of Liberia, in the home of my friend with cancer, here with us in our worship this morning.

"For where two or three are gathered in my name, I am there among them." That's the promise that I'm willing to hang my hat on. That's the promise I'm willing to stake my life on.

1. Sermon: September 7, 2014. Readings: Exodus 12:1–14; Psalm 149; Romans 13:8–14; Matthew 18:15–20.

NINE

Glory

Often, at the end of a long Sunday, I'll take a peek at the gospel reading for the next week, not to study or analyze it in any way, but just to see what's coming. On this particular Sunday, I soon wished I hadn't. The coming text was from the Gospel of Mark.

Then he began to teach them that the Son of Man must undergo great suffering, and be rejected by the elders, the chief priests, and the scribes, and be killed, and after three days rise again. He said all this quite openly. And Peter took him aside and began to rebuke him. But turning and looking at his disciples, he rebuked Peter and said, "Get behind me, Satan! For you are setting your mind not on divine things but on human things."

He called the crowd with his disciples, and said to them, "If any want to become my followers, let them deny themselves and take up their cross and follow me. For those who want to save their life will lose it, and those who lose their life for my sake, and for the sake of the gospel, will save it" (Mark 8:31–35, *NRSV*).

I groaned a little as I read it. That's going to be hard, I thought. Those who want to save their life will lose it; and those who lose their life will save it. It would be a challenge, first to make sense of the text, then to figure out what to say about it. But that was a task for the days to follow, not a Sunday evening. So I set it aside, turned on the TV and settled into the couch to watch the Academy Awards presentation.

The Oscars captured my attention more than usual in 2015 mostly because I had seen quite a few of the nominated movies. It had been an outstanding year in the movies for a physics geek. There were movie biographies of two of the greats, Alan Turing *(The Imitation Game)* and Stephen Hawking *(Theory of Everything)*, and a third movie, *Interstellar*, which relied on the theoretical equations of Einstein's general relativity to generate a wormhole that was integral to the storyline. But it wasn't just the physics. *The Imitation Game* was an eye-opener, revealing in Turing's tragic story the appalling way that society has criminalized, "pathologized," and persecuted homosexual people, as recently as 60 years ago in Britain and still today in more than 70 countries around the world. Then there was *Selma*, the inspiring story of Martin Luther King Jr. and the fateful crossing of the bridge in Selma, Alabama, one of the key moments in the fight for civil rights for African Americans. Coming as it did in the aftermath of the Ferguson shooting and riots, *Selma* was a timely reminder of the history of the civil rights movement and of the ongoing issues of racial injustice in the United States and beyond. In my mind, *Selma* was the most moving film of 2014. I wasn't the only person disappointed to see it receive just two Oscar nominations. The trending #OscarSoWhite hashtag expressed the frustration of millions. At least its theme song was nominated, and song performances are often the best part of the televised presentation. So though I don't usually find these award shows to be all that interesting, I had hopes that this year might prove an exception. At worst, it would be a good way to relax and unwind after a long day. At best, there was always the preacher's hope that a widely watched cultural event might yield some sort of homiletical nugget.

And so I sprawled on the couch, half-snoozing my way through the presentations and perking up whenever one of the nominated songs was performed. Midway through the evening, the screen went blue and a little Lego figure wiggled its way to the foreground. "Everything is Awesome," it sang, the theme song from *The Lego Movie*. Recording artists Tegan and Sara slid into view, dwarfed by Oscar statuettes, singing under a bright flashing rainbow. With a spin of the rainbow, the stage was filled in quick succession by high energy rappers in bright blue tuxedos, dancers in costume doing head-spins and even someone in an awesome possum body-suit, all with pulsing lights, pumping beats, and giant images projected on the video screen behind. It was pure Hollywood: over the top and totally in keeping with the ridiculously optimistic lyrics of the theme song. Life is good because everything is awesome. We're living our dream. It was fun. It was colourful. It was a burst of energy. It was totally superficial. I sunk back into the couch.

After what seemed like a long time and a lot more talking, Octavia Spencer, the Academy Award winner from Montgomery, Alabama, stepped up to the microphone. The mood changed as she recalled the year that the Oscar presentations had been postponed, in 1968, four days after the assassination of Dr. Martin Luther King Jr. Then she introduced a song that "speaks to the troubles that continue to this day." The theatre went dark as John Legend sounded the first chord of *"Glory"* on the grand piano. With soaring melody and spoken word Legend and Common pointed to the mountaintop and brought us to our feet. And when the chorus of voices sounded "Glory" for the final time, there was a moment of glory that lingered, and I wasn't the only one whose cheeks glistened.

SERMON

"Glory"[1]

"For those who want to save their life will lose it; and those who lose their life for my sake, and for the sake of the gospel, will save it."

That's a hard statement. But there's no avoiding it. It is central to our faith, too central to our faith to avoid or ignore. It is at the core of who we are, or who we're called to be as followers of Jesus, as disciples. It's there, right at the turning point of the gospel, right after Peter declares Jesus as Messiah, right at the moment when Jesus sets his face towards Jerusalem. There is no avoiding it.

"For those who want to save their life will lose it; and those who lose their life for my sake, and for the sake of the gospel, will save it."

This is a hard teaching. It's hard in two ways. First, it's hard to understand. It is, at least on the surface, a paradox, something that we have to wrestle with in order to get a grip on it. Second, the more we begin to understand, the more we glimpse its meaning, the more that we *do* get a grip on it, the more we realize that this is so hard to do. Because it goes beyond our normal human ways. It calls us into the divine; it calls us toward something greater than ourselves.

Last Sunday evening, I watched the Oscars on TV. I was more interested this year than I am most years because I had managed to watch a good number of the nominated movies. And so I watched the awards show, as I imagine many of you did, hoping for a moment of inspiration. Mostly, I was disappointed. But there was one moment that inspired me, one moment that lifted me up during the Oscars. Tegan and Sara's performance of "Everything is Awesome," the theme song from *The Lego Movie*, was not that moment.[2]

Now, my apologies to those of you who might like *The Lego Movie*, or Tegan and Sara, but that performance was not awesome.

That was taking a silly little song, and then adding more and more fluff to it in a futile attempt to make it awesome. Add more dancers. Add more colour, more lights, a rainbow. Spin on your head. Spin again, throw in an awesome possum and some Lego statues.

There was nothing inspiring there. Sure maybe it was fun, and that's okay once in a while, but it was superficial, all style with no substance, no meaning, no purpose. That's not the life I want. There's got to be more to life than that. Forget "Awesome." I want a life that means something. I want to be lifted up. I want to be inspired by a purpose so great that I'm willing to put my life at its service. I want a glimpse of glory.[3]

Minutes later the stage darkened and the black and white image of a soaring metal bridge filled the screen. The first chord sounded from the piano, and John Legend began to sing *Glory*.

"One day when the glory comes, it will be ours, it will be ours."

That's what Jesus was talking about. Glory. The march across the bridge in Selma in 1965. "If any want to be my followers, let them deny themselves and take up their cross and follow me." Self-giving for the sake of others. Sacrificial love. Denying ourselves for a good greater than ourselves. For glory. God's glory.

Martin Luther King Jr. and many other courageous black Americans marched across that bridge in Selma in order to obtain the civil rights for black Americans that many of us take for granted. The first time they tried to get across the bridge they were brutally attacked by state troopers. One man, Jimmie Lee Jackson, was murdered as he tried to protect his mother from a beating. But the marchers persevered, at great risk to themselves. People of all colours and races flooded into Selma to support the marchers, and a few days later, 25,000 people marched from Selma to the Alabama state capital of Montgomery and forced the U.S. government to pass the Voting Rights Act of 1965.

It was a time of great fear and suffering. It was also a moment, a foretaste, of glory.

"For those who want to save their life will lose it; and those who lose their life for my sake, and for the sake of the gospel, will save it."

You want to know what Jesus is talking about? Well, it doesn't look like the clip we saw from "Everything is Awesome." It doesn't look like playing it safe. It doesn't look like getting more and more stuff. It doesn't look like being entertained, prosperous, happy, or successful. I mean, "what will it profit you to gain the whole world and forfeit your life?" No. The life God is calling us to looks a lot more like that bridge in Selma, a lot more like the sacrificial love demonstrated by the people who walked across that bridge at great personal cost and risk. That's how you save your life. That's how to really live, to live the abundant life that God is calling us to.

Every time we set aside a want of our own in order to satisfy the genuine need of someone else, we experience a moment of glory.

We know that to be true. We do it naturally as parents when our baby cries in the middle of the night. We find glory in those moments when we give up our claims to power and strength and even a good night's sleep in order to serve others. Sometimes it comes naturally; much of the time it is hard and requires a God-given strength.

For each of us, our Selma will look different. Sacrificial love and service to others take many shapes and forms, some of which will indeed require great courage.

But make no mistake about it. This is the core of our faith. This is what we are all about.

"For those who want to save their life will lose it; and those who lose their life for my sake, and for the sake of the gospel, will save it."

We are called to glory.

1. Sermon: Lent 2 – March 1, 2015. Readings: Genesis 17:1–7, 15–16; Psalm 22:22-30; Romans 4:13–25; Mark 8:31–38. The homily presented in this chapter incorporates video. Readers are encouraged to watch the videos of "Everything is Awesome" and "Glory" when they are referenced as footnotes.
2. Video: The 2015 Academy Awards performance of "Everything is Awesome", theme song from *The Lego Movie.* www.youtube.com/watch?v=mwjUm8Lz7Y4 (accessed March 4, 2017).
3. Video: The 2015 Academy Awards performance of "Glory," theme song from the movie *Selma.* www.youtube.com/watch?v=H9MKXR4gLjQ (accessed March 4, 2017).

TEN

How Dare We?

Easter is a challenge. The proclamation that a dead person has been raised and is alive is always going to be a challenge. But for preachers, Easter is a challenge in a different sort of way. It is the most important day of the Christian year, the day when church attendance peaks. That alone burdens preachers with a self-imposed weight of expectation. It also means that there will be a preponderance of people whose faith commitment is unknown: visitors, family members, and those who may only attend church once or twice a year. Statements that we may take for granted on another Sunday require more context on Easter Sunday.

There is also a timing issue. Easter is invariably preceded by Holy Week: Palm Sunday one week prior, various Holy Week observances on Monday through Wednesday, and then the Triduum – Maundy Thursday, Good Friday, the Easter Vigil for some, and then Easter Sunday. For me, the timing creates an emotional offset: the very days that I start thinking about how I am going to preach the joy of Easter fall amidst the most sombre observances of the Christian year. It always feels a little weird.

In 2014, that weird feeling, the dissonance between the liturgies at which I was presiding and the Easter homily which I was preparing, was compounded by a funeral. Ten days before Easter, the Hon. Jim Flaherty died tragically of a heart attack at age 64. Flaherty had been Canada's minister of finance for eight years, and had played a key role in guiding Canada's economy through the financial crisis of 2008. He was well-liked, and well-respected. Just three weeks before his death, he had resigned as finance minister to return to the private sector and to spend more time with his family, including his triplet sons. It was not to be.

The honour of a state funeral was extended to Jim Flaherty by Canadian Prime Minister Stephen Harper. The funeral took place on Wednesday of Holy Week at St. James Cathedral in Toronto, Ontario. That seemed appropriate. Though Flaherty was born of an Irish Catholic family, his church home was All Saints Anglican in Whitby, Ontario, where he had served as a churchwarden in the 1990s. The state funeral was attended by more than 1,500 people. The streets around the cathedral were closed to traffic and many sat outside on the church grounds, watching the televised service on large screens.

It was an emotional affair, broadcast live on radio and television across the country, with extensive news coverage both before and after. There was a real sense of tragedy, of a death that came too soon, of a life cut short just as a new phase was about to begin. The bell tolled and a single bagpipe played as the casket was brought into the church. Moving eulogies by Flaherty's wife Christine Elliott and their three sons brought many in attendance to tears. The presider, Archbishop Colin Johnston, offered words of hope to those in attendance and to those listening across the country: "St. Paul says to us that we are not to weep as those without hope. Amidst grief we have the comfort that God is present with us. Easter is God's last word, not Good Friday."[1] And as the final words of the eulogies echoed through the cathedral, the congregation was invited to stand and sing, and I was struck by the transformation, and the audacity, of the moment.

Praise, my soul, the King of Heaven,
To his feet thy tribute bring.
Ransomed, healed, restored, forgiven,
Who like me His praise should sing

Praise him! Praise him! Alleluia!
Praise the everlasting King.[2]

Sitting at home on the living room couch, watching as events unfolded on TV, allowed me a measure of detachment. As an observer, I was struck by the fact that at the very moment when the congregation was at its most vulnerable in the face of death, at the moment that we were reminded of the power of death to cut our lives short and plunge us into grief, the congregation stood as one and, with a powerful voice, proclaimed its praise to God in song. It was a corporate act of defiance. A determination, to borrow a line from Bruce Cockburn, to kick at the darkness until it bleeds daylight. How is it that we dare to do such a thing?

An existentialist might respond that we choose to do so. Though we may have no reason to sing praise in the face of death, though we know it's not a rational act, we simply choose to do so precisely because it is an act of defiance. But for Christians there is more to it than that. We believe that death is not the end. That all appearances to the contrary, death has been overcome and defeated. That nothing, not even death, will separate us from the love of God. And so we stand and sing praise to God, even in the face of death, because we are an Easter people.

The reading for Easter Sunday was from the Gospel of John.

Early on the first day of the week, while it was still dark, Mary Magdalene came to the tomb and saw that the stone had been removed from the tomb. So she ran and went to Simon Peter and the other disciple, the one whom Jesus loved, and said to them, "They have taken the Lord out of the tomb, and we do not know where they have laid him." Then Peter and the other disciple set out and went towards the tomb. The two were running together, but the other disciple outran Peter and reached the tomb first. He bent down to look in and saw the linen wrappings lying there, but he did not go in. Then Simon Peter came, following him, and went into the tomb. He saw the linen wrappings lying there, and the cloth that had been on Jesus' head, not lying with the linen wrappings but rolled up in a place by itself. Then the other disciple, who reached the tomb first, also went in, and he saw and believed; for as yet they did not understand the scripture, that he must rise from the dead. Then the disciples returned to their homes.

But Mary stood weeping outside the tomb (John 20:1–11a, *NRSV*).

SERMON

How Dare We?[3]

On Wednesday afternoon I watched the state funeral for the Honourable Jim Flaherty, which took place at St. James, the Anglican Cathedral, in Toronto. There were 700 people inside the cathedral and many more outside, all gathered to mark the death of this man. The funeral began, as many do, with eulogies. As these were spoken, there were visible signs of grief. There were tears and there were shaky voices.

When the eulogies had finished, the whole assembly stood as one and sang, "Praise, My Soul, the King of Heaven." And I thought to myself as I watched, "How is it that when we gather to mark a death we dare to sing such praise to God?"

The lower level of this church is the home of Centre 454, a day program for those who are homeless or who live in poverty. Centre 454 is one of five community ministries of our diocese. You may know that the tag line, or motto if you like, of our community ministries including Centre 454, is "Choose Hope." Every day, there are men, women, and children who walk through the doors of Centre 454, and Cornerstone, and The Well. Often these are people who have been beaten up by life. People who suffer from mental illness and addiction. People who are trying to escape abusive relationships and violence. People who have been worn down by poverty and have been told over and over again that they're no good. When these people walk through our doors with the deck of life stacked against them, how is it that we dare to tell them to choose hope?

Earlier this year, we worked our way through Jesus' Sermon on the Mount and we heard Jesus say that we should love our enemies and pray for those who hate us. We talked about that and we acknowledged that it would be hard for us – that we might never be able to do it. But we took it seriously. How is it that we even dare to take seriously let alone agree with someone who tells us to love those who hate us?

On another Sunday, we heard about the time that Peter asked Jesus, "if a brother or sister sins against me, how often should I forgive? Should I forgive as many as seven times?" Jesus responded, "Not seven times, but, I tell you, seventy times seven." When we tell this story, how is it that we dare to think that Jesus is the one who's making sense rather than Peter?

We dare to say and do these things because we are an Easter people.

We dare to say and do these things because we are a people who believe that life is stronger than death, that love will overcome hate, that hope is greater than fear, that forgiveness is better than judgment, and that the suffering and grief of this life is real but it is not the ultimate reality.

We believe these things because we are an Easter people. Easter changes everything.

It certainly did for Mary Magdalene. As our gospel reading opens this morning, Mary is not yet an Easter person. She is still living in the aftermath of Friday. The events of the past week have unfolded for her with dizzying speed: the false hope of Palm Sunday and the triumphal entry into Jerusalem, the gathering storm as the enemies of Jesus plot against him, the pain and grief of witnessing the gruesome death of the man she loved, the fear and uncertainty of what comes next. It is still dark when Mary makes her way to Jesus' tomb on that Sunday morning. She goes to the tomb, I suppose, in an attempt to hang on to something of what she has lost. But when she sees that the stone has been removed from the tomb, she's confused; she panics and she runs to get help. The body has been stolen. It is perhaps the final indignity – that her enemies would even take away his dead body, the only reminder of him that she has left. She runs to get help. But when Peter and the other disciple have come and gone, Mary is left alone once more, weeping.

Have we not, will we not, all experience such things at some point in our lives?

And yet I believe that it is in these moments that Jesus calls to us and speaks our name.

Jesus calls us out of grief and fear and confusion and sadness, and into an encounter, into a relationship with the living God.

Mary hears that voice. She hears her name. And that changes everything.

At the beginning of our liturgy this morning, we began by singing "Jesus Christ is risen today," and in our opening words we proclaimed, "Christ is risen, the Lord is risen indeed, alleluia!" That's what we do as a community of faith.

But Mary's proclamation is much more personal. "I have seen the Lord." She is proclaiming a personal encounter, a life-changing experience, a life-giving relationship. She is talking about something that matters for her in a very personal way.

Sometimes we make the mistake of thinking that Easter is about something that happened to Jesus. Yes, Jesus was raised. But Easter is about something that happens to *us*, to you and to me. Something that gives us the courage, the strength, the sheer audacity to declare that life is indeed stronger than death, that love will indeed overcome hate, that hope is indeed greater than fear, that forgiveness is indeed better than judgment, and that the suffering and grief that we experience are not the last word.

None of this is self-evident nor is it obvious. In fact, there are many who look at the evidence of history and of the world around us who think that we are fools for believing such things. There are those who think that only a fool would mark a death by singing hymns of praise to God. That only one who is naïve would urge a broken person to choose hope.

But we are an Easter people. We do these apparently foolish things because we are people of faith. We believe in the power of life, love, hope, and forgiveness because Christ was raised from the dead, and appeared to Mary, and then to Peter, and then to the 12, and then to more than 500 brothers and sisters. We believe because these first witnesses risked their own lives to tell others about what they had experienced first-hand. And we believe because we continue in a whole variety of surprising and exciting and confusing ways to experience Christ as real and alive in our own lives. I have seen the Lord.

We are an Easter people.

1. "Anglicans remember Jim Flaherty as man of faith, integrity" by Stuart Mann, April 17, 2014, www.toronto.anglican.ca/2014/04/17/anglicans-remember-jim-flaherty/ (accessed March 4, 2017).
2. "Praise, My Soul, the King of Heaven." Words: Henry Francis Lyte, 1834.
3. Sermon: Easter 2014. Readings: 1 Corinthians 15:1–11; Psalm 118:1–2, 14–24; Acts 10:34–43; John 20:1–18.

ELEVEN

Doubt, Singularities, and the Big Bang

We live in a secular age. What makes our age secular is that the context for belief has changed. So writes philosopher Charles Taylor in his 2007 book *A Secular Age.*

"The shift to secularity in this sense consists, among other things, of a move from a society where belief in God is unchallenged and indeed, unproblematic, to one in which it is understood to be one option among others, and frequently not the easiest to embrace."[1]

Simply put, when it comes to belief, there are alternatives. In our time and place, no matter what it is that we believe or disbelieve, the likelihood is that we will know intelligent, reasonable people who disagree with us. Indeed, they may be our friends and family.

As people of faith, this is the context in which we find ourselves. As preachers, this is a reality not only for ourselves but for the people to whom we speak. And the season in our church year when this changed context for belief matters most is Easter. In one of the earliest written accounts of the events of Easter, St. Paul wrote in his first letter to the church in Corinth, "if Christ has not been raised, then our proclamation has been in vain and your faith has been in vain" (1 Corinthians 15:14). And yet despite its centrality, we know that people wrestle with the Christian proclamation of Jesus' resurrection from the dead. Some simply write it off as impossible. That's nothing new; most of our predecessors in the first century did the same. But even those who believe in the resurrection wonder what really happened and some struggle to reconcile their belief with the world view of modern science and the skepticism they encounter all around them. What do you say about Easter in a world of doubt and evidence-based decision making?

However a preacher wishes to address the question of doubt, Easter Sunday is not the time to do it. Easter Sunday is the great celebration of the Christian year. The resurrection of Christ is not just presumed, it is proclaimed over and over again, in spoken word and song. It just isn't a good time for a preacher to dwell on doubt. But we don't have to wait long, because on the second Sunday of Easter, our weekly cycle of Sunday readings introduces us to the very person whose name has become synonymous with doubt for almost 2,000 years: Thomas, the one called the twin, also known as "doubting Thomas."

But Thomas (who was called the Twin), one of the twelve, was not with them when Jesus came. So the other disciples told him, "We have seen the Lord." But he said to them, "Unless I see the mark of the nails in his hands, and put my finger in the mark of the nails and my hand in his side, I will not believe."

A week later his disciples were again in the house, and Thomas was with them. Although the doors were shut, Jesus came and stood among them and said, "Peace be with you." Then he said to Thomas, "Put your finger here and see my hands. Reach out your hand and put it in my side. Do not doubt but believe." Thomas answered him, "My Lord and my God!" (John 20:24–28, NRSV).

SERMON

Doubt, Singularities and the Big Bang[2]

Evidence-based decision making. Sounds like a good thing doesn't it? Isn't that why we argued about bringing back the long-form Canadian census in our recent federal election? We spend billions of dollars each year doing research and gathering evidence so that we can make good decisions. So why is it that when Thomas declares that he needs to see the evidence, we label him as a doubter and hold him up as an example of what not to do for 2,000 years? It hardly seems fair.

You know the story. Thomas isn't there on that first Easter evening when Jesus comes and stands among the disciples gathered behind the locked doors of the house in Jerusalem. So when he gets back, and when the others tell him, "We have seen the Lord," Thomas will not believe them. Emphatically he exclaims, "unless I see the mark of the nails in his hands, and put my finger in the mark of the nails and my hand in his side, I will not believe." Show me the evidence, and then I'll decide.

On that night, Thomas is in the minority. The other disciples, more than ten of them, *they* believe. They have come to faith. They proclaim the resurrection. Thomas doesn't buy it. He questions. He doubts. He wonders.

On that night, Thomas was in the minority. But if Thomas was to return today, I have to think that he'd be in the majority. We live in an age of skepticism. Of doubt. Of questioning. Of evidence-based decision making. If Thomas were to show up in the city of Ottawa today, he'd be in the majority. If Thomas were to show up in this church today, I think he'd be in the majority.

That's not to say that we don't believe in the resurrection of Jesus. I believe in the resurrection. But my faith in the resurrection has been a hard-fought battle in the midst of doubt, questions, and wonder. I know that dead bodies stay dead. I've looked at the evidence. My faith is not limited by, but it definitely makes room for, evidence-based decision making.

One of the things that I noticed about today's gospel reading is that the community of the disciples, the nascent church if you like, makes room for Thomas and his doubts and questions. When Thomas declares that he will not believe on that first Easter day – when he basically tells them by implication that either they're lying or they're delirious – the community could have told him to take a hike. That he no longer belonged. But they don't. A full seven days later, seven days that must have seemed like an eternity to Thomas, he's still with them, he's still welcome, he still belongs. And finally, on the evening of the eighth day, he gets the evidence he's looking for and he comes to believe.

And then something important happens. Thomas, the doubter, the skeptic, the one with the questions, the latecomer to the party, Thomas is the one who then makes the boldest and most profound confession of faith in Jesus contained in the whole Bible: "My Lord and my God!"

For some of us, faith comes easily. For others, like Thomas, faith is more of a process, a battle even. We need the freedom to ask questions. We need to be able to express our doubts. Doubts are okay. Doubt is important. Indeed, if we don't have any doubts, we may not be taking our faith seriously enough.

I mean, think about what we confess: that there is a Creator who made this vast universe we live in, and that this Creator cares deeply and passionately about our individual lives, our ups and downs; and that because the Creator loves us so much he became incarnate in the human person of Jesus, who died like every human does, but was raised and appeared in bodily form to his disciples. If we're serious about this, and we are, we have to acknowledge the possibility of doubt.

Here at St. Albans we have four core values: "welcome, connect, explore, and serve." Nobody bats an eyelid at three of those four core values. But people notice that having "explore" as a value is different. Sometimes people ask me about that. I tell them that we value exploration because for many people, in order to come to a bold, vigorous, and vibrant faith, like Thomas did, they need to be able to express their doubt. They need the freedom to ask questions. They need the time and space to examine the evidence. They need the possibility of being like Thomas, doubting and questioning, and yet still be embraced by the community. For a week. For a year. For as long as it takes.

Because what we are talking about here is not trivial. Nor is it an academic or intellectual exercise. When we come to faith, when we come to believe in the resurrection, that's not the end of it. We are then called to proclaim it. And proclaiming the resurrection is always an act of defiance.

We get that in the story from Acts that we read this morning. A few months after Thomas declares, "My Lord and my God," Peter and John are arrested and put in jail for publically proclaiming the resurrection. In the reading we just heard, they are brought before the council and the high priest. The high priest forbids them to speak of the resurrection of Jesus, telling them "we gave you strict orders not to teach in this name." But in defiance of the authorities, Peter and the apostles answer, "We must obey God rather than any human authority. The God of our ancestors raised up Jesus, whom you had killed by hanging him on a tree."

Proclaiming the resurrection is an act of defiance. Christians throughout history, Christians today who are persecuted for their faith – in Iraq, in North Korea, in Lahore, Pakistan[3] – know this only too well, sometimes at the cost of their lives.

Our proclamation here in Ottawa will not cost us our lives. But it is still an act of defiance. In proclaiming the resurrection, we proclaim that despite all the evidence to the contrary, God is in charge and is renewing and restoring this world as we speak. We proclaim, against the tide of modern secularity, that this universe is more than a material world. We proclaim that the cosmos and even our own individual lives have meaning and purpose – God-given meaning and purpose. We proclaim that love is stronger than hatred, that life is stronger than death.

None of these things can be proven. They are confessions of faith. Faith-based statements. Though we look for evidence, like Thomas, the truth is, we live by faith.

I have questions. I have doubts. I wonder about things. I look for evidence. I'm a lot like Thomas.

But I live by faith. I live by faith in the resurrection of Jesus. Why do I believe in the resurrection?

Because I rely on the testimony of witnesses, a great chain of witnesses throughout history reaching back to Mary Magdalene, the first to say, "I have seen the Lord." A great chain of witnesses that includes those disciples in the upper room, and the others to whom Jesus appeared and who witnessed to that appearance, whose testimonies have been passed down from generation to generation.

I believe in the resurrection because I rely on the historical evidence. The historical evidence that those first witnesses, against all the odds, succeeded in turning the world upside down by their defiant proclamation, a proclamation that ended up costing most of them their lives, a proclamation that lives on in the life of the church throughout the world today.

I believe in the resurrection because the resurrection of Jesus and all that it implies makes sense of my experience of the world. My intuitive sense of the spiritual dimension of our universe. My observations of the profoundly relational dimensions of human life. Stuff in my life that I interpret to be experiences of the divine. My relationship with God.

I know that dead bodies stay dead, and so therefore the resurrection of Jesus must have been a singular event that is outside the normal way this universe operates. My training is after all, as a scientist, a physicist. I get evidence-based decision making. But ironically, it is physics that has taught me about singularities, doubt, and the limits of knowledge.

When Isaac Newton formulated his rightly famous theory of gravity, he refused to publish his work or to discuss it broadly for decades. Why? Because though he realized that this idea of gravity explained all of the evidence, he had no way of explaining or understanding how one massive object could interact with another massive object at a distance in a vacuum, as the theory of gravity requires. It seemed like, to quote Newton's own words, "a great absurdity." But eventually, like Thomas, he pushed through his doubt and hesitation and he looked at the evidence, and two decades after he first discovered it, he published that great absurdity, his theory of gravity.

In the 20th century, physicists, looking at the evidence, looking at the mixture of elements in our world, the movement of stars, and patterns of radiation, have concluded that they could best explain this physical evidence by the hypothesis of a singular, non-repeatable event that defies the known laws of physics of our universe, and that occurred outside of space and time as we know them. They call this singularity the Big Bang and believe it to be the explanation for how our universe came to exist in the form that we know it. I believe in the Big Bang theory, even though it is a singularity that defies the known laws of physics of our universe. Sure, there's an element of faith there, but that's where the evidence is pointing. Sometimes it's the singularity that makes the most sense.

Many of us have doubts and questions. If you do, then Thomas is your guy.

Thomas, with his doubts and questions, with his propensity for evidence-based decision making, would be welcome here at St. Albans. Those of you who are modern-day Thomases, you are welcome here too.

Bring your doubts, ask your questions, wrestle with your faith, and do it here, in the embrace of a loving community. My hope is that through this process of exploration, just like Thomas, you too will come to a bold and vibrant and vigorous faith and that together we will be able to defiantly proclaim the resurrection.

Alleluia, Christ is risen. The Lord is risen indeed. Alleluia.

1. Charles Taylor, *A Secular Age* (Cambridge: Belknap Press, 2007), 3.
2. Sermon: Easter 2 – April 3, 2016. Readings: Acts 5:27–32; Psalm 150; Revelation 1:4–8; John 20:19–31.
3. On Easter Sunday, March 27, 2016, at least 69 people were killed and 300 injured in Lahore, Pakistan, in a suicide bombing that targeted Christians celebrating Easter: www.nytimes.com/2016/03/28/world/asia/explosion-lahore-pakistan-park.html (accessed March 4, 2017).

TWELVE

Dagobah, Emmaus, and the Recognition Problem

"May the Force be with you."
"And also with you."

It is a little known event in the church year – one that occurs only every seven years or so. You won't find it in any of the standard lectionaries or liturgical calendars. Yet for devotees of a certain movie franchise and their friends on social media it generates a surprising amount of internet traffic and enthusiasm: *Star Wars* Sunday. Sunday, May the fourth. May the fourth be with you.

Even though the first *Star Wars* movie came out when I was in my late teens, it wasn't until much later that I became a passionate fan of the original trilogy. In the mid-1990s, I travelled to San Diego to attend an Air Traffic Management trade show. On my off-day, I decided to go to the air and space museum. There was a special exhibit on "The Mythology of Star Wars," which explored the ways in which George Lucas and his movie trilogy had been inspired by the myriad expressions of the heroic myth chronicled by Joseph Campbell in his classic text *The Hero with a Thousand Faces*.

Campbell identifies a common thread, which he calls the "monomyth," in the diverse mythologies of the Greek, the Norse, and many other civilizations. In its simplest form, this monomyth tells the story of a hero who emerges or is called forth from his or her ordinary world and daily life into a new world of wonder. If the hero accepts the call, he or she will face tasks and trials and encounter strange forces. At its most intense, the hero may face a severe challenge, which, if survived, results in new powers and, just as importantly, new self-knowledge. The hero must then decide whether to return to the ordinary world from which he or she came, and, upon return, whether to use these newly acquired powers to help others.

It has always been the middle stage of the journey that captures my imagination – the descent into the depths, where the outer journey mirrors the inner journey, where the hero's battle with the external forces of the mythological world reflects their interior battle with their own weaknesses and demons. Psyche's voyage to the underworld in her quest for her lost lover, Cupid; Frodo's descent into the mines of Moria, or his confrontation with Shelob, the giant spider in *The Lord of the Rings*; Katniss' struggle in *The Hunger Games* – these and many more stories are not mere mythological fantasies. They are also coming-of-age stories to which many of us can relate.

In *Star Wars*, the descent into the depths begins when our hero, Luke Skywalker, crash-lands his spaceship in a swamp on the planet Dagobah. Luke is the one who has been called out of his ordinary life as a young farmer on the planet Tatooine, and told by his mentor, Obi-Wan, that he must go to Dagobah to seek out Yoda, the Jedi master who will train him in the ways of the force. But as Luke picks himself out of the swamp, Yoda is nowhere to be found. The only one Luke meets on Dagobah is a small green creature hobbling through the swamp, who speaks with an odd syntax.

In 2014, "Star Wars Sunday" fell on the third Sunday after the first full moon following the spring equinox, otherwise known as the third Sunday of Easter. Fittingly, our gospel reading for this Sunday landed us in the depths, on the road of trials, or as it is known in Luke's gospel, the road to Emmaus. It is the middle stage of the "hero's journey," the moment when two disciples, Cleopas and his companion, are at their lowest point, overwhelmed by grief and despair, and ready to walk away from the adventure to which they have been called. It is at that moment that they encounter someone with the power to change their lives, if only they can recognize this stranger that they meet on the way.

Now on that same day two of them were going to a village called Emmaus, about seven miles from Jerusalem, and talking with each other about all these things that had happened. While they were talking and discussing, Jesus himself came near and went with them, but their eyes were kept from recognizing him. And he said to them, "What are you discussing with each other while you walk along?" They stood still, looking sad. Then one of them, whose name was Cleopas, answered him, "Are you the only stranger in Jerusalem who does not know the things that have taken place there in these days?" (Luke 24:13–18, *NRSV*).

SERMON

Dagobah, Emmaus, and the Recognition Problem[1]

There is a problem that I've noticed as I've listened to our Easter readings these past three Sundays – a recurring problem that runs through the texts. I call it the "recognition problem."

We saw it first with Mary at the tomb on Easter morning, when she turns and Jesus is standing there, but she thinks that he must be the gardener. We saw it in our reading last week, when Jesus appears in the locked room with the disciples, but they don't know who he is until he shows them his hands and side. We see it in our reading today, when Jesus joins Cleopas and his companion on the road to Emmaus. They don't recognize him.

And if recognition is a problem for these first people to whom Jesus appears in bodily form, how much greater a problem is it for those of us who come later! We don't get to see Jesus' resurrection appearances. We don't get to hear him call our name the way Mary does. We don't get to see the wounds on his body like Thomas does. And that is a problem.

Do we recognize the risen Christ in our lives? Is God with us? How do we recognize God's presence? Can we, in our own time, see and experience the divine in the events and activities of our lives? Because let's be honest. When we proclaim "Alleluia Christ is risen, the Lord is risen indeed" during the Easter season, there are a lot of people who don't see it. There are many people, within the church and outside the church, who have a hard time recognizing God as alive and active and present in their day-to-day lives. In fact, I would go so far as to say that the recognition problem is the biggest challenge facing most Christians. We don't want to just tell stories about the past. We want to *experience* something that is alive and real and that makes a difference in our lives *today*.

The recognition problem is so important that for centuries it has been, and continues to be, a common thread that weaves its way through our stories and mythologies. One of the reasons I am a big fan of *Star Wars* is that I love how the movies reveal in a new way the classic themes of the human story. One of my favourite scenes from *The Empire Strikes Back* is set in a swamp on the planet Dagobah. Our hero, Luke Skywalker, has been sent to Dagobah by his mentor Obi-Wan Kenobi to become a Jedi knight. Luke is on a quest. He must learn the ways of the Force. To do so, he will have to become a disciple of Yoda. So with his droid R2D2, he sets off in his spaceship. But when he gets to Dagobah, his ship crashes into a swamp. Luke, bemoaning his fate, begins to salvage some equipment from the ship and carries bits and pieces to a dry clump of ground in the midst of the swamp. All he has to do is find Yoda, but that doesn't look like it will be easy. Suddenly, Luke gets the feeling he's being watched. He spins and points his gun at a small green creature cowering in the shadows.

"Away put your weapon I mean you no harm. I am wondering – why are you here?" asks the little creature.

"I'm looking for someone," replies Luke

"Looking? Found someone you have I would say, hmmm," replies Yoda, laughing.

But Luke doesn't recognize Yoda. He's looking for a great warrior, not this annoying little swamp creature. Yoda grabs Luke's food and starts playing with his stuff. Before long, Luke's had enough.

"Can you move along little fellow, we've got a lot of work to do."

"No, no, no, stay and help you I will. Find your friend, hmm?"

"I'm not looking for a friend, I'm looking for a Jedi master."

"Oooh, Jedi master. Yoda. You seek Yoda. Take you to him I will."

And Yoda, still unrecognized, sets off through the swamp, inviting Luke to follow.

So why doesn't Luke recognize Yoda? Well, Luke is looking for something, but he doesn't really know what he's looking for. He thinks he's looking for a great warrior, a Jedi Master, and he has certain expectations of what that should look like. It certainly doesn't look like a short ugly creature hobbling around in a swamp with a cane. Luke is too proud to accept help when offered, and he suffers from his own biases and preconceived notions.

It's easy to laugh, and perhaps there are a few lessons we can learn from Luke's failure to recognize Yoda. But I also want to acknowledge the very real pain that occurs when people aren't able see or experience God in their lives. When your life crash-lands and you are alone in the swamp and God is not there, this is a real problem. That is where the two disciples on the road to Emmaus find themselves as our gospel story begins this morning. "We had hoped that Jesus was the one to redeem Israel. But they crucified him." Our gospel begins as a story of crushed dreams, lost hope, and broken hearts. Perhaps the only thing worse than having no hope is to have once hoped, but then to hope no more. "We had hoped...."

Throughout the ages, men and women have experienced the absence of God as a painful moment in their lives. St. John of the Cross called it the "dark night of the soul." C. S. Lewis and Mother Teresa both write about their "dark nights." It is an agony I expect is made even more acute in this Easter season, as we listen to shouts of "I have seen the Lord" all around us.

So why does Luke tell us this Easter story? After all, he had a few to choose from. As Luke mentions at the end of the text, there was another resurrection appearance to Simon Peter that happened on this same day just down the road in Jerusalem, but he chose not to write about that one. Instead, gives us this one, the one that happened on the road to Emmaus.

Why this story? I think it's because Luke understands the importance of the recognition problem and because he wants to make us a promise.

I'd like you to do something. Look at the service booklets that we have been following this morning, and tell me this. What are the four main section headings for our time of worship together?

The four section headings are We Gather as a Community, We Proclaim the Word, We Celebrate the Eucharist, We Are Sent.

That is the basic four-part structure of the liturgy we celebrate together every Sunday morning. Now, think back to what you just heard about the disciples on the road to Emmaus. It begins with Jesus joining the two disciples and walking with them. They gather as a community. Then, after the disciples tell Jesus what has happened, Jesus interprets the scriptures for them, beginning with Moses and all the prophets. He proclaims the Word to them. When that is done, and the day is nearly over, the disciples urge Jesus to stay with them and they share a meal together. Jesus takes the bread, blesses it, breaks it, and gives it to them. Or as we might say, they celebrate the Eucharist.

It is in the breaking of the bread that they recognize Jesus, and realize how their hearts were burning within them, even before that moment of conscious recognition. They get up and race back to Jerusalem to find the others and tell them what has happened. They are sent.

We gather as a community. We proclaim the Word. We celebrate the Eucharist. We are sent.

It is no coincidence that the four movements of Luke's story and the four movements of our worship here this morning are the same. Luke's gospel was shaped by the worship of the early Christian community, and our worship has been shaped for centuries by Luke's gospel.

This is no coincidence. It is, rather, a promise. The promise Luke is making to those of us who experience the recognition problem. The promise Luke is making to those of us who are broken-hearted, the promise that Luke is making to those of us who are experiencing the dark night of the soul, is this: in Christian worship, we will encounter the risen Christ. In the gathering of the community, in the proclaiming of the word, in the breaking of the bread, in the sending, Christ is present.

Christian worship is a solution to the recognition problem. It's not the only solution. We can experience and recognize God in all sorts of ways in our lives. Nor is worship a magical solution; it's not going to give you a guaranteed experience of what you expect to see every time. But our worship together each Sunday morning is an opportunity to recognize the presence of God in our midst, and that's something that we learn to do together. It is in this gathering that broken hearts can become hearts that burn with joy within us, and that we can dare to say together, "We have seen the Lord."

1. Sermon: Easter 3 – May 4, 2014. Readings: Acts 2:14a, 36–41; Psalm 19; 1 Peter 1:17–23; Luke 24:13–35. The original homily included a video clip from *The Empire Strikes Back*: www.youtube.com/ watch?v=rlKoiJu9TsQ (accessed March 4, 2017).

THIRTEEN

The First Stone

The stones passed from hand to hand as we sang, eventually making their way to me. I slipped them into my pocket, as yet unaware of the impact they were to have. There is a cross on the Camino de Santiago where these stones would eventually come to rest. That cross is one of many on the Camino, made of bent iron mounted high on a wooden post. The Cruz de Ferro is distinguished by its elevation, located high on top of a mountain crossing. It is surrounded by millions of small stones piled around its base. But it is best known as the spiritual peak of the Camino Frances, the ancient pilgrimage route from St. Jean Pied-de-Port in France to the cathedral of Santiago de Compostela in northwestern Spain, the legendary burial place of St. James the apostle, known in Spanish as Santiago.

The Camino had captured my imagination several years before by way of a series of books, conversations, and movies, the most popular of which was *The Way* starring Martin Sheen. When a good friend decided to embark on the pilgrimage, I knew about Cruz de Ferro, and the Sunday before he left I explained the ritual of the stones to our congregation, and arranged to have a stone passed from hand to hand for my friend to take with him. It is said that a stone left at Cruz de Ferro represents an unburdening, the casting off of whatever it is that holds us back or weighs us down, whatever it is that prevents us from being the people that God created us to be.

The practice of pilgrimage has exploded in recent years. Perhaps it's the increasing ease with which we can travel; perhaps it's an antidote to the complexification of our daily lives; perhaps it's a spiritual awakening. Whichever the case, more and more people are embarking on pilgrimages, and one of the most popular is the Camino de Santiago. As recently as the 1980s, there were fewer than 5,000 people who completed the Camino each year; by 2015 over a quarter million pilgrims from around the world would receive their *compostela*, the certificate of completion of the Camino de Santiago. That's less than the half-million who walked the route each year in the Middle Ages, but it's still a dramatic increase over the past 30 years.

Why walk the Camino? That's the question that starts many a conversation on the way to Santiago. You wake at daybreak, dress, splash some water on your face, put your possessions into your pack and start walking. At some point, when your pace puts you in synchrony with another walker, you might start with hello and *Buen Camino* (which literally means "good path" and is generally understood as "have a good journey"), but sooner or later someone asks, "So why are you walking the Camino?" The responses can be as varied as there are individuals, but rarely are they trivial or superficial. There's something about spending a day walking, and then multiple days in succession, that deepens thoughts and gives rise to good conversations. It could be the simple rhythm of the walk. Perhaps it's the gradual change in one's perception of time. Or maybe it's simply that we have time, something that often seems to be in short supply at home.

My pilgrimage piqued the interest of many, including our St. Albans community. Even before I arrived home, the men's breakfast group invited me to talk about the Camino the first Saturday morning that I was back. I decided to tell them the story of the second stone.

"You remember how on the Sunday before Guylaine (my wife) and I left on our pilgrimage we passed two stones around the church for

us to take to Cruz de Ferro. As it happened, Guylaine already had a
stone which had been given to her, so I ended up with two stones.
Which turned out to be a good thing, because as I made the trek up
the steep slope that leads to Cruz de Ferro, with one stone in each
hand, both came to be of significance. Let me tell you about the
smaller stone, the one in my left hand, the one I call the 'second
stone.' Some of you may know that I've been doing some writing.
That hasn't been easy. It's hard to find the time to write when you've
got a full-time job. It's even harder to self-identify as a writer. There's
this nagging doubt as to whether you've really got something to say
that others might find worth reading. There's the reality that getting
your work published is hard, and making a living from writing is
even harder. There's the vulnerability associated with putting your
words out there for others to read, and the inevitability of
disagreement and criticism. For all these reasons, you might say
that as a writer, I was in the closet. But as I was walking up the
mountain to Cruz de Ferro, on a beautiful blue-sky day, it felt like I
was being called to come out of that closet. The stone in my left hand
came to represent all the fears and vulnerabilities that were stopping
me from writing. So when I got to the foot of the cross, standing on
that pile of stones, I dropped my stone and let go of all those obstacles,
and I became a writer.

"Now it was early in the morning when we passed Cruz de Ferro
and there was still a long day of mountain walking in front of us.
Towards the end of the day it was hot and the sun no longer felt like
a friend. I stopped and sat on a rock under the shade of a gnarly old
tree. I reached for my phone. Normally I keep my phone tucked
away while walking, but I was tired, and there was a GPS app on
the phone that would let me know how far I still had to walk to make
it to the next village. To my surprise, there was a new message in
my email. My phone must have picked it up without my knowledge
as we walked through a Wi-Fi zone earlier in the day. I tapped on
the email, and there was a message from the publisher that I'd sent
my book proposal to months ago: 'Dear Mark, Sorry for the delay,

but we'd like to publish your book.' That's the story of the second stone."

We continued to talk, and to eat. But inevitably someone asked, "So what about the first stone?" To which I replied, "For that one, you'll have to come back tomorrow."

SERMON

The First Stone[1]

Guylaine and I spent the last month in northern Spain, walking the ancient pilgrimage route to Santiago de Compostela, the Camino. You may recall that on the Sunday before we left, John told us about one of the sites along the Camino, Cruz de Ferro. On that Sunday, you passed two stones from hand to hand and gave them to us to take to Cruz de Ferro and leave there. This morning I want to tell you the story of one of those stones. It's not a linear story, because the Camino has a way of messing with your sense of time. Things happen, thoughts emerge, words are said. Making connections and drawing out meaning happen in their own time, with little respect for chronological order.

Every journey has a dual nature. There's the journey outwards, travelling to distant lands, encountering different cultures, making new friends, and going to places you've never been before. And then there is the journey inward, the journey that takes you to destinations within yourself, some of which may be familiar but some of which may also be places you've never been before. It is the mirroring of these outward and inward journeys that makes walking the Camino a powerful and rewarding experience.

One of the insights I had on the Camino was that Jesus spent most of his life walking, and especially during his final three years, walking with his disciples, his companions along the way. There's something about walking that lends itself to spiritual exploration. Perhaps it's the rhythm. Perhaps it's because we have time. Perhaps it's that mirroring of the outward and inward journeys that I experienced. In today's gospel, Jesus is walking with his disciples, somewhere in the rural part of Galilee. And, as they walk, they ask him questions. "What's God like?" they ask. "What do you mean when you say that the kingdom of God has come near?"

And so Jesus points to a field where a man is sowing seed and says, "the kingdom of God is as if someone would scatter seed on the ground, and it grows, and he does not know how." They walked some more. Then Jesus spots a bush with yellow flowers that produces a tiny seed. "You want to know what God is like? Imagine a tiny mustard seed sown upon the ground which grows into the greatest of all shrubs." And on they walk.

That's what we do on the Camino. We walk. We talk. We think. We look. We listen. We smell. One morning, I walked with Laura, an American woman. We started talking. I asked her a question. There was a moment's hesitation. I said to her, you can give me the long answer if you want, we have time. And so she did. She reached way back in her life and spent the next hour or two telling me her story.

Some people walk the Camino for specific reasons. They might be between jobs. They might be asking the "What am I going to do with my life?" question. They might be trying to leave a relationship behind or figure out whether to embark on something new.

I went on the Camino without a specific agenda, at least not one that I was consciously aware of. In fact, I intentionally spent the first week trying *not* to bring any agenda to my thoughts. Instead, I wanted to allow the walking and the encounters to open me up. It was only later and as my walking was drawing to an end that I realized and was able to articulate that my Camino *did* have a purpose, and that was to come to know God and to know myself more deeply. Maybe that's the underlying purpose of any pilgrimage. Which brings me to the story of the stone you gave me.

Cruz de Ferro, the iron cross, is located at the highest point of the Camino, some 1,500 metres above sea level. It is a tall slender cross, not particularly impressive when compared to some of the beautiful crosses encountered along the way. What *is* impressive is the large pile of stones at the base of Cruz de Ferro, as high as a house, with each stone having been left by one of the millions of pilgrims who walked the Camino before us. The tradition is that each stone represents a letting go of something, the unburdening of a weight carried by the pilgrim but now released. That tradition is grafted onto an even more ancient tradition that tells us that it is upon the mountaintop that we encounter God.

That morning I began the ascent to the mountaintop, some seven kilometres away. Halfway there I stopped for breakfast in Foncebadon, the last village before Cruz de Ferro. As I was leaving, I opened my pack and took out the two stones you gave me. I carried one in each hand as I walked. It was a beautiful, clear, blue-sky morning. I knew that the stones I carried were sacred, having been blessed by you as you passed them hand to hand; they carried your intentions and thoughts. I hadn't actually given any thought as to what those stones would mean to me, what it was that I might need to let go of, what sort of unburdening. But walking the Camino has a wonderful way of giving you the thoughts you need when you need them. As I walked those last few kilometres, it became quite clear to me what the stones were for. As for the one in my left hand, the smaller one, well, that's a story for another day. The larger stone in my right hand came to represent all the things that prevent me from experiencing forgiveness.

Now that came as a total surprise to me, because I didn't think I had an issue with forgiveness. Heck, I've even preached sermons on God's grace, on how God forgives us, how God sets aside all of our issues and brokenness and misdemeanors and loves us, now, just as we are. But it was as if a voice said to me, "Sure, you know all about forgiveness in your head, and your theology of grace isn't bad at all. But have you experienced it?"

And I remembered there was that thing that I still feel badly about, that I still try to justify every so often rather than just accept forgiveness. And then, the more I thought about it the more I realized that I spend a lot more time and energy trying to justify myself than I do accepting forgiveness. I like being right; I like being good. In fact, I like being better than other people. My competitiveness, my tendency to compare myself to others, my desire for self-justification, my pride in accomplishments: as I walked up the mountain, I realized, or you might say, I was taught, that all of these things actually get in the way of forgiveness and create an inability in me to accept at the deepest level that I am forgiven. And so, I would have to let them go.

Forgiveness is an ancient theme on the Camino. In the Middle Ages, the reason that pilgrims walked the Camino was to receive forgiveness. About a ten-day walk before the end of the Camino there is an old church in a village called Villafranca that dates from the Middle Ages. The church has a door called the *Puerta de Perdon* – the door of forgiveness. Mercy. Pardon. Pilgrims who were too sick to make it over the Galician mountains to Santiago were able to receive forgiveness at the *Puerta de Perdon*. These days we often smirk at the superstitions of the Middle Ages and ridicule the church for its practice of selling indulgences. The notion that forgiveness is obtained by walking 700 kilometres or more to see the relics of a saint seems silly to us, and, at face value, it is also bad theology. God's grace is freely given. Whatever was needed for God to forgive was done through the mystery of the cross. Walking hundreds of kilometres on bruised and blistered feet adds nothing to what God has done.

But despite this theology of grace, how many of us truly experience forgiveness? How many can forgive themselves and others? How many of us struggle with doubts about self-worth? How many still experience guilt? How many of us know in our hearts that we are loved, with no strings attached? How many are still captive to the brokenness of shattered dreams and crumbled relationships?

God wants to unburden us from all these things. Forgiveness, grace, is freely given. But what does it take for us to *receive* it, to *accept* it, to *experience* it deep in the core of our being? Perhaps the ancient beauty and mystery of the Camino is that the outward journey really *does* mirror the inward journey that we need to make to come to an acceptance of forgiveness. When a pilgrim of the Middle Ages came to know that she or he was forgiven at the *Puerta de*

Perdon, was it because of the path that had been walked, or was it something much deeper? Perhaps it was because over the course of those many kilometres that person had come to know God as gracious and forgiving, full of steadfast love and mercy, and the gift of forgiveness had been accepted a little bit deeper into their heart with every step they took along the way. Perhaps that's the deeper meaning of the Camino as a quest for forgiveness.

We'll never really know the experience of a 12th-century pilgrim. But 21st-century pilgrims also need to receive, experience, and come to know the grace of God. Perhaps it's more important to make the journey and to arrive at this destination than to have a theologically sound explanation of how to get there.

So when I climbed to the top of the pile of stones at Ferro de Cruz, I dropped my stone. I let go of all that it had come to represent, all the things, known and unknown, that prevent me from experiencing forgiveness.

I came down off the stone pile. I waited a bit. I wondered if anything was going to happen. I put my pack on and I started walking again. Then I remembered the hug.

A couple of days earlier, we had arrived at the *albergue,* the hostel, after a long 30-kilometre-plus day of walking. My feet were sore and my ankle was swollen. Just off to the side of the *albergue* lobby there was a massage therapist with her table, working on tired pilgrims. Guylaine said to me, "Maybe you should get some work done." So I booked a time and went to the therapist. She introduced herself with a shake of the hand as Sylvia, asked me what was wrong, and went to work, mostly on my feet and ankles, and my shoulders which were groaning a bit from carrying my pack. Afterwards, she took the time to explain to me what I needed to do to care for my feet and the best way to tend my blisters. Then to my complete astonishment, she wished me *Buen Camino,* and gave me a hug. A big, long, firm hug. It surprised me. It moved me. It felt great.

As I walked away from Cruz de Ferro, I remembered the hug. In fact, I experienced that hug again, fully present once more in that moment. It was a hug that said "You are loved." A hug that said "You are my beloved child; with you I am well pleased." It was what we in the church might call a sacrament, an outward and visible sign of an inward and spiritual grace. And I came to understand that it was God who was hugging me through those arms, letting me know, in the embodied language that I can understand at a gut level, that I am forgiven, and that I am loved.

Having experienced that, I suppose I will never be quite the same again.

And that is the story of the first stone.

1. Sermon: June 14, 2015. Reading: Mark 4:26–34.

FOURTEEN

Something More

We go on pilgrimage because we are looking for something less. Less, in that we are afforded the opportunity to set aside much of the baggage of our daily lives. Literally, that means that we travel with a small pack, just six or seven kilograms depending on how full one's water bottle is – one change of clothes, some toiletries, a sleeping bag, rain gear, a guide book, a notebook, and a pen. That's about it. But less also means fewer distractions. No job, no home to look after, no computer. More time spent in the present, less in the past or future. You wake, you walk, you stop, you eat, you walk, you think, you stop, you eat, you talk, you wash, you write, you look after your feet, you sleep. A pilgrimage provides the opportunity for less.

But most of the pilgrims that I walked with were also looking for something more. That elusive, sought-after something more was expressed in a wide variety of ways. There were the concrete expressions: what career should I pursue, should I embark on this new relationship, should I leave home and family to start over in a new corner of the world? There were people at a crossroads in life: where do I go now that my loved one has died, my spouse has left me, my children are grown up, my job has ended? Then there were people whose articulation of the something more was less concrete: how can I live a life that's more meaningful, more peaceful, more joyful? How can I leave behind a life that's become a bore, stuck in a rut? For some, a minority, the quest for something more was clothed in explicitly religious terms; for many, it was a yearning to lead a more spiritual life. Their own intuition told them that the craving they experienced for meaning and purpose in their lives could be satisfied neither by human invention nor social convention.

Some come to the Camino hoping for an experience: a blazing insight, the presence of God, even a miracle. On my first day, the trail climbed steeply out of France up the Pyrenees mountains into Spain. The sky was clear, a deep blue, and the sun was hot overhead. I was resting by a water fountain that had been used by pilgrims on this route for centuries when I heard an exclamation of joy and surprise from the trail below. A Scandinavian-sounding woman was obviously delighted at the sight of the fountain. Seeing me she blurted out in English, "It's a miracle. I was so thirsty, and I was thinking how much I needed water, and then I looked up and there was this fountain. It's my first day on the Camino, and already I've been given a miracle." We could debate whether the discovery of a centuries-old water fountain is a miracle. You might want to call it a coincidence. You might be more generous and call it a sign. But clearly she had been looking for something. And though hers might have been an extreme case, most pilgrims are indeed looking for something; an experience of some sort, a taste of something different, an escape from the daily grind.

The quest for something more takes time and it takes persistence. Maybe that's why pilgrimage is a good fit. Pilgrimage takes time. Pilgrimage takes persistence. In fact, it obliges us to be persistent; it forces us to keep going, to stay on track, to stick around, to keep walking. Even when you want to quit, the buses in rural Spain are few and far between and the schedules sporadic and not always reliable. Once you're on the way, you're committed and you keep walking, sometimes because you have no choice.

It's easy to overlook how much walking Jesus did with his disciples as we read our scriptures. Their ministry from village to village in Galilee, and then the journey on to Jerusalem were very much a pilgrimage, often, as we're told, with nowhere to lay their heads. The disciples didn't follow the yellow arrows of the Camino; they followed Jesus. They were on a quest for that "something more," and it involved a lot of walking and talking and persistence along the way. Their persistence was illustrated by one of the mid-summer gospel texts we read soon after I returned from the Camino.

"Those who eat my flesh and drink my blood abide in me, and I in them. Just as the living God sent me, and I live because of the living God, so whoever eats me will live because of me. This is the bread that came down from heaven, not like that which your ancestors ate, and they died. But the one who eats this bread will live for ever." He said these things while he was teaching in the synagogue at Capernaum.

When many of his disciples heard it, they said, "This teaching is difficult; who can accept it?" ...

Because of this many of his disciples turned back and no longer went about with him. So Jesus asked the twelve, "Do you also wish to go away?" Simon Peter answered him, "Lord, to whom can we go? You have the words of eternal life. We have come to believe and know that you are the Holy One of God" (John 6:56–60, 66–69, NRSV adapted).

SERMON

Something More[1]

In May this year, I walked the Camino de Santiago, the ancient pilgrimage route across northern Spain, to the city of Santiago de Compostela, where the remains of St. James are found. It's a long walk. You might wonder why there are so many people who take a month or more out of their lives and are willing to walk such long distances, often in great pain because of blisters and bruised feet. If you ask these pilgrims why they are there, why they are walking, as I often did, you get a wide variety of answers, responses that are as varied and as unique as the individuals you encounter on the way. But if there is a common theme that seems to emerge from these conversations, it is this: most of the people walking the Camino are, in one way or another, looking for something. They are looking for something *more*. They want to know if there is more to life than their present circumstance is giving them, if there is more to life than what society or their culture or their family is telling them.

Is there more to life than this? And if there is, how do we get it? We're not talking about mere survival here. We're talking about more than that. We're talking about life in its fullest, about abundant life, about the life we were created for and meant to live. Maybe, if we dare, we're talking about a life so rich and so full of love and energy that it will even burst the usual constraints of death, space, and time. How do we get that? How do we live that sort of life?

That's the question that Jesus is responding to in our gospel reading today. The question for us in return is whether we believe him or not. We've spent five weeks now reading through the sixth chapter of the Gospel of John, beginning with Jesus' feeding of the 5,000. Usually it's called the "bread of life discourse," because it begins with loaves of bread and continues with Jesus proclaiming himself as the bread of life. But in the final dozen verses or so of this chapter, which we heard this morning, a funny thing happens. The word "bread" disappears, and the word that takes its place as the focal point of the dialogue is "life." Because it's not about bread. What's at stake here is life.

You might recall that when we first started talking about the feeding of the 5,000, I pointed out that in the Gospel of John, Jesus never performs any miracles. The great acts of power that he does are not miracles, they are *signs*. They point to a bigger truth, a more challenging truth. Jesus has fed the crowd of 5,000 people with five loaves and two fish. The next day, the crowd seeks him out again, hoping for more food. But Jesus responds to their questions by pointing them towards the bigger truth. He wants to move the people from a search for bread to the search for life. But the offered path from bread to life passes through a series of claims that Jesus makes about himself and God. And that's where many in the crowd get stuck. In response to the desire for more bread, Jesus says, "I am the bread of life," taking for himself the divine name "I am" revealed by God to Moses. He tells the crowd that just as God sent manna to their ancestors in the wilderness, it is "the living God who sent me." He claims to be from God, the bread "which came down from heaven," and that he will ascend once again to where he was before. These are big claims, claims which John summarizes in the prologue to his gospel, when he writes of Jesus as the Son of God, the Word who was God, who became flesh and dwelt among us.

If you believe this, you will have life – abundant life, eternal life, that life in its fullest sense that we all in one way or another are looking for. That's what's at stake. The something more that we've been searching for appears to be within sight, within our grasp.

But first you have to get past the claim.

And most of the crowd, and many of Jesus' own disciples can't do it. They just can't do it.

"This teaching is difficult, who can accept it?" The people are offended, even scandalized.

Why is accepting this claim so hard?

For two reasons, I think. First, because it is an affront, a shocking challenge to our understanding of God. And, second, because it calls us into a relationship that may seem too close for comfort.

How do *you* picture God?

The people listening to Jesus would have been caught off guard by Jesus' claims. They knew God as YHWH, the almighty God who, with a mighty hand and outstretched arm, had brought their slave ancestors out of Egypt and into the land promised by God, establishing a covenant with them and making them God's people.

They knew that the dwelling place of YHWH was the temple in Jerusalem. Not that the temple could contain God – as Solomon says in our Old Testament reading, even the heavens and the highest heaven cannot contain the Lord. Yet it is the temple that is filled with the glory of the God and that is the place of God's presence on earth. To these people, the claim that Jesus, this man from Nazareth standing in front of them, was actually the Son of God, the human person in whom the presence of God dwelt – well, that was a scandalous claim.

I suppose that after 2,000 years Jesus' claim seems less scandalous to us today, though no less daunting. But how do you picture God?

We might think of God as the Creator of the heavens and the earth. Perhaps we use philosophical concepts: God as supreme being, as almighty, omnipotent, omniscient, and omnipresent. Perhaps you think of God as Spirit: invisible, present, breathing life into every aspect of our physical world. Whatever understanding you have, how do you reconcile it with the claim that, in the words of St. Paul, in the human person of Jesus, the fullness of God was pleased to dwell?

The claim that Jesus makes is difficult because it challenges our understanding of who God is.

But the second reason Jesus' claim is hard is because we are being called into a relationship, a relationship with this God who is found in the person of Jesus. Jesus offers us life, but it is not life all wrapped up in a box and handed over to us with no strings attached. It is the life we seek; but it is found through relationship with him.

That's what Jesus is trying to convey when he uses the image of eating. That's what the gospel writer John means when he uses the words believing and abiding. We are being invited into a relationship, with all that a relationship in its fullest sense entails: commitment, fidelity, intimacy, mutuality, vulnerability, knowing and being known, and sacrificial love – all the good stuff and all the hard stuff.

Do you think you can handle the intimacy of a relationship with God? Can you handle the commitment of a relationship with God?

Do you get why most of the crowd disappears?

I have to think that Jesus is disappointed when the crowd – and not just the crowd, but also many of his disciples – turn away and leave him. He turns to the 12, his closest friends, and says to them, "Do you also wish to go away?"

It is Peter who speaks. "Lord, to whom can we go? You have the words of eternal life. We have come to believe and know that you are the Holy One of God."

Why does Peter choose to stay when others decide to leave?

I expect that Peter is a seeker, just like the rest of us. He, too, had been looking for something more, searching for that abundant life that each of us wants. I suppose that's why he left his fishing boat to follow Jesus in the first place. And, as he followed Jesus, as he walked with him, day after day, month after month, as their relationship grew, Peter must have experienced something. He must have had at least a taste of that abundant life that he was seeking.

So when Jesus offers that life through relationship with him, for Peter that amazing claim has a ring of truth about it. Jesus has the words of eternal life; that's what Peter has come to believe because he's experienced it, at least in some measure. And so he's going to stick around. I admire that persistence.

And maybe, like Peter, that's what we need to do too. We too need to stick around, to walk with Jesus long enough to experience the life he has to offer. Kind of like a pilgrimage.

1. Sermon: August 23, 2015. Readings: 1 Kings 8:22–30, 41–43; Psalm 84; Ephesians 6:10–20; John 6:56–69.

FIFTEEN

It's Time

The first church conversation about sexual orientation that I remember took place in the 1970s, when I was as a teenager. A story started circulating in our local church about a priest in one of the parishes of the diocese who was gay, and that seemed to be causing a problem. I didn't learn any of the details. The adults at the time didn't think to make me part of the conversation. But when I overheard later that the matter was to be resolved by allowing the priest to continue, but requiring him to be celibate, that made sense to me at the time. In the 1970s, society was coming to an awareness based on scientific research that homosexuality was an orientation, not a choice. At the same time, the traditional teaching of the church that gay sex was wrong went relatively unchallenged. A decision not to condemn someone for being the way that God made him, but to require him to refrain from doing something the church considered a sin seemed a reasonable approach to my young self. It was only later that I realized that this stance contained within it the seeds of contradiction.

Some 40 years later I was elected by that same diocese as a delegate to the 2016 General Synod of the Anglican Church of Canada, the national meeting of the church, which takes place every three years. The prominent item on the agenda was whether to change the marriage canon to provide for same-sex marriage. The General Synod of 2013 had put this on the agenda for 2016 by passing a resolution to that effect. In the interim, a commission had been struck to examine the matter, to consult broadly, and to produce a theological report, which it did. But despite the advance warning, despite the work of the commission, despite the importance of what was before us, we seemed to be sleep-walking towards General Synod 2016, with limited engagement across the country. All that changed in the last days of February 2016, just four months before the Synod was scheduled to take place. That's when the House of Bishops issued a statement; based on discussions at their most recent meeting, the motion to change the marriage canon at General Synod was not likely to pass in the Order of Bishops by the required two-thirds majority.

The bishops' statement came like a bolt of lightning into a sleepy pond. Advocates for changing the marriage canon came to life. Social media was engaged, letters were written, videos produced. People questioned why we were choosing a legislative route that required the high bar of a two-thirds supermajority in each of the three orders of bishop, clergy, and laity, in two consecutive synods, to proceed. Lawyers looked more closely at the existing marriage canon and concluded that it did not actually preclude same-sex marriage. Various individuals and groups issued statements in response to the bishops' statement. Some even decided to read the report produced by the Commission on the Marriage Canon, *This Holy Estate*.[1] But most importantly, LGBTQ Anglicans put themselves forward as living examples of what it looks like to be a faithful Christian *and* lesbian, gay, bisexual, transgender, or queer. They posted pictures of their families; they wrote about their experience. They talked about their hurts and their hopes – hopes of getting married or simply of being fully included in the church that they loved and that was such an important part of their lives. They helped many of us to understand that the decision we were about to make wasn't about *them*; it was about *us*.

The vote on the marriage canon was to take place on the fourth day of General Synod, on the Monday. In the days leading up to this, we worshipped, and we listened to presentations. We dealt with other business, and we ate together. We talked a lot about marriage and sexuality and our LGBTQ friends. We talked in table groups and we talked as "neighbourhood" groups of 25 or so. Those things required hours of attentive and exhausting listening. There were reports of difficult, even bullying conversations in some groups, but in my group the conversations were open, respectful, and help-ful. There were poignant stories and there were appeals to scrip-ture and tradition. There was division, and there was fear about how that division would play out. Hanging over everyone's head was the knowledge that we were at a knife's edge – no one knew which way Monday's vote would go.

The motion to change the marriage canon to provide for same sex-marriage finally came to the floor of General Synod on Monday afternoon. The lineups at the floor microphones made it immediately apparent that the debate would extend into the evening session. The first order of business was an amendment to the main motion that would give dioceses the opportunity to opt into same-sex marriage rather than being allowed to opt out as provided for by the original motion. The opting-in amendment, which only required a simple majority, passed with 60 percent of the vote. We proceeded to the main motion, as amended. A total of 60 speakers stood to address the motion. Some spoke of their own experience as gay or transgender Christians within the church. Others noted that in their parishes they were just beginning to have conversations about sexual orientation, and that moving too quickly would be divisive. Some reminded us that we had been talking about human sexuality in the church for 40 years and that it was time to move ahead, to move on, and to allow the church to bring its attention and its voice to other pressing matters. Some quoted scripture or appealed to tradition to justify their opposition to homosexuality. In a few instances, the tone was harsh.

The break for supper afforded an opportunity for hallway conversations. There was a concern among several of us that the debate was veering away from the actual motion at hand. We agreed that this needed to be addressed on the floor. But most of the people

I was talking with had already spoken. "You do it," they told me. I hadn't planned to speak, thinking that it was better to make space for people from the LGBTQ community to make the case for the motion. But when the debate resumed, I joined the lineup on the floor. It took a good half-hour to get to the microphone.

"Members of Synod, in my neighbourhood group, we had really good conversations, helpful conversations that reminded me that we come from very different contexts. For some people, this conversation about sexuality has been going on for 40 years. For others, this is a new conversation. Where I come from, in my parish in urban Ottawa, moving forward with this motion on same-sex marriage is both extremely important and urgent. I believe that it's time. For me, this is a gospel imperative, an imperative that is grounded in the love of Jesus that is revealed to us in our scriptures.

"But many have said that they need more conversations, more study, more time. I get that. I understand. I've been there. I've been wrestling with this for almost 40 years. The present resolution, as amended, is designed to allow for more time, and to make space for disagreement while still moving forward. First of all, this is a first reading. Our constitution, in its wisdom, provides for a three-year period of discussion and conversation prior to a second reading of the motion at General Synod in 2019. Then, once three years have passed, the opting-in amendment we have adopted allows each diocese through its bishop to determine its own course, its own process, its own timing. That includes the option of not doing anything in response to this motion. We need to make space for each other. This resolution, as amended, is a way of making space for each other."

Late in the evening, the vote was called. Each of us had been equipped with electronic clickers so that the votes could be counted and recorded electronically. We voted in three waves, one for each of the three voting orders of bishop, lay, and clergy. I looked down for the green light as I pressed "1" for yes, hoping my electronic clicker wouldn't screw up. The meeting chair, Archbishop Fred Hiltz, the primate, reminded us that there was to be no applause when the results were announced. Then the results were displayed on the screen. I looked first at the bishops' tally: 26 to 12 – 68 percent in favour. It passed! But my joy was short-lived. Laity: 72 percent. Clergy: 66.23 percent. There was a moment's hesitation at the head table. People around me started to whisper "It passed!" But the mathematicians among us knew better: 51 in favour, 26 against. We had failed to achieve the two-thirds majority required for approval in the order of clergy by one vote.

The chair announced the failed result to stunned silence in the room. The young transgender person sitting opposite me broke into silent tears. The rest of us at our table just sat there in disbelief. With all the attention that had been paid to the outcome in the order of bishops, we were stunned that the motion had failed in the order of clergy. It was already late at night. General Synod moved into evening prayer. But the conclusion of evening prayer did not conclude our evening as it normally would. The house was still in session, and as the prayers ended, one of the bishops moved to the microphone.

"Your grace, there are people concerned that their clickers may not have functioned correctly. Given the closeness of the vote, I would move that there be a recount."

There was a brief consultation at the head table.

"A recount is not possible, since with electronic voting there are no paper ballots to recount. It would, however, be possible to ask for a reconsideration if that is what you wish."

A reconsideration would mean doing the vote over again. The motion to reconsider would require a two-thirds majority of the house as a whole to pass.

"I move a reconsideration then."

A flurry of activity ensued, as those who had been moving to the doors returned to their seats and texts were sent to colleagues who had already left the room. The vote to reconsider received only 64 percent in favour. There would be no repeat of the vote. The evening session was over. But our day was not yet done.

Many of my parishioners at St. Albans, and many Anglicans across the country, had been watching events unfold live on streaming video. Many more people were following on social and mainstream media. The newspaper headlines the next morning would say that the vote had failed. Some would consider leaving the church as a result. But there was more to the story than that, and so a number of us wanted to get word out immediately that night, to provide context and to frame the narrative. We had anticipated this possibility, and statements had already been drafted. Within minutes of the close of session, I posted the following on our St. Albans Facebook page:

Dear Friends,

Today at the General Synod of the Anglican Church of Canada, a strong majority of delegates (70 percent) voted in favour of a resolution to change the marriage canon to provide for same-sex marriage, including a strong majority in each of the orders of bishop, clergy, and laity. The resolution did not, however, receive the two-thirds majority in the order of clergy required for changing a canon (it fell short by one vote). Therefore, we will not be proceeding by means of a legislative change at this time. It is now the responsibility of each bishop to determine the appropriate pastoral response in his or her diocese.

Some will be disappointed by the result of today's vote. But I believe that the Spirit of God is on the move in all of this, and that God will provide a way forward. I believe that this is an important moment that will allow us to move forward with the full inclusion of LGBTQ people in the life, leadership, liturgies, and sacraments of our church here in the Diocese of Ottawa and beyond, and I'm looking forward to hearing from Bishop John Chapman as to how this may unfold. Please keep our bishop and all those affected by today's decision in your prayers.

Grace and Peace, Mark

I hit "send." Then I immediately went to assist Bishop John with a final proofreading of his pastoral response. I knew what it was going to say. Bishop John had already shared with our Ottawa delegation his thoughts, both in the event of a yes vote and a no vote. His pastoral response would be to proceed immediately with same-sex marriage in the Diocese of Ottawa. And Ottawa was not alone. It was almost midnight. I went to the bar in the lobby of the hotel. To no one's surprise, it was packed with synod delegates at the end of a long and stressful day.

As I approached the bar, my friends from Saskatchewan called me over. We had spent time together in our neighbourhood group. Most of them had in good conscience opposed the motion on same sex-marriage, and they knew that I was an advocate. Anticipating my disappointment, they felt terrible, and they offered to buy me a beer, which I gratefully accepted. We sat and talked into the wee hours of the morning, colleagues united by something bigger than any vote or disagreement.

Waking up the next day was not easy. I grabbed my phone, scanned my social media feed, switched to my laptop and typed out one more post.

Good morning from #GS2016. #ItsTime. Last night we voted with an overwhelming majority to proceed with same-sex marriage. The headlines this morning will say that this vote failed because it didn't get the two-thirds majority in each order required to change the marriage canon. But this morning it is becoming clear that we are now in a new reality. Already the bishops of Ottawa, Niagara, and Toronto have announced a process for proceeding with same-sex marriage, with more to come. By the end of the week, most Canadian Anglicans will live in a diocese where same-sex marriage will soon be celebrated. We may well look back on today as a historic milestone in the full inclusion of our LGBTQ friends. They have been more than patient.

With that, I trudged downstairs to do my duty as a synod delegate and attend to those items on the agenda for the last day of our assembly. I thought that General Synod 2016 was done with same-sex marriage. Little did I know what was about to unfold.

Arriving in the assembly hall I found that the first order of business had been pre-empted by a new motion. In the wake of the defeat of the same-sex marriage vote the previous evening, a motion had been put forward to reaffirm General Synod's 2004 resolution affirming the integrity and sanctity of committed same-sex relationships. I groaned inwardly as I saw a lineup start to form at the microphones. There was no need to repeat the previous night's debate. Thankfully, the first speaker moved to close debate, which was approved, and the motion was then approved with 78 percent in favour.

On a point of order, another speaker asked the chair when the record of the previous night's vote on the marriage canon would be made available. The response was that, in the normal course, it would be released with the minutes of General Synod, which would take several months. A mild grumbling could be heard in the hall. There were still doubts about our electronic voting system floating around the room. We moved on to other business.

By mid-afternoon of that final day, we were just about ready for motions of thanks and a presentation by the host diocese of the next general synod, when one more time a delegate moved to the microphone on a point of order. This time the delegate was more insistent, making a motion that the voting record of the motion on the marriage canon be released immediately. The motion was approved and during one of our few breaks, about 30 minutes later, the record of the vote was released onto the electronic tablets that had been provided to each of the delegates.

When we returned from the break, the agenda indicated that it was time for the customary motion of thanks. It was not to be.

The bishop of Quebec stepped to the microphone, accompanied

by two priests of the diocese. He introduced them, and the first addressed the chair.

"I am concerned to report that I voted in favour of changing the marriage canon to provide for same sex-marriage, but the voting record which has been released indicates that I did not vote."

The second stepped forward to report the same omission.

A muttering broke out around the assembly hall. We knew the math. The resolution had failed by one vote in the order of clergy. Either of these missing votes would have made the difference. But how would the chair proceed? No one doubted the word of these two, but there was no physical evidence of their vote. Did they press their electronic clickers within the prescribed time? Perhaps this was the electronic equivalent of a spoiled ballot?

Then another speaker reached the microphone. "Your grace, I counted the actual number of votes in the electronic record which was released, and the actual result is 52 clergy in favour, not 51 as was announced yesterday." The speaker was asked to approach the chair to show his work, and then the head table huddled with the subcontractor who was responsible for the e-voting system. I went back to my tablet and quickly added up the vote, confirming what had been said. The General Secretary addressed the house. It turns out that there had indeed been an error. The General Secretary himself had been entered into the database as a lay delegate when he was, in fact, a member of the clergy. Moving his vote to its proper place in the order of clergy would give the resolution the required two-thirds majority in each of the three orders.

"They're going to have to declare that the resolution passed," I whispered to the person sitting next me.

The head table was seized with caution, feeling perhaps the gravity of the moment. The chancellor repeated the facts and the sequence of events several times, buying time, making sure that everything was clear, creating space to make sure that no more revelations or surprises would come to light.

Finally, Archbishop Fred Hiltz, the chair, spoke. "The resolution to change the marriage canon has been carried."

Once more there was stunned silence in the house. Most of us were emotionally exhausted by the long days, the high drama of the previous night's debate and vote, and the lack of sleep. Just when we thought the emotional rollercoaster had come to a halt, the rails shifted unexpectedly under our feet and we were falling again.

Some were angry. A number of people stood and left the room. For those who had opposed the motion and thought it had failed, this was a shocking turn of events. For those of us who had supported the motion, there was no immediate celebration, because we had learned the previous night what it feels like to lose. Though my head told me this was a good thing, I felt terrible in the immediate aftermath of the reversal. I tapped out a quick tweet on my phone: "#GS2016 Recount! The motion to change the marriage canon is declared carried! #ItsTime!" Then I left the hall during a brief break to find a quiet corner. I returned to the hall for the final Eucharist, but I didn't go back to my table. I found my friends from Saskatchewan, the ones who had bought me a drink the night before, and joined them at their table for our closing worship.

That Sunday, back in Ottawa at St. Albans, we had our celebration. We celebrated our LGBTQ friends and members. There was a rainbow cake, the church was packed, and it was my first Sunday back after a three-month sabbatical and then General Synod. Normally I preach from the lectionary, the prescribed cycle of scripture readings, but on this occasion I decided to select the readings myself: the account of the Jerusalem Council of 50 A.D. from the Acts of Apostles, where the difficult decision was made to set aside Jewish circumcision and food laws in order to welcome non-Jews into the church (Acts 15:1–12); John's gospel account of the new commandment that Jesus gives at the Last Supper: "Love one another as I have loved you;" (John 15:12–17); and Paul's clarion call for inclusion found in the third chapter of his letter to the Galatians.

For in Christ Jesus you are all children of God through faith. As many of you as were baptized into Christ have clothed yourselves with Christ. There is no longer Jew or Greek, there is no longer slave or free, there is no longer male and female; for all of you are one in Christ Jesus. And if you belong to Christ, then you are Abraham's offspring, heirs according to the promise (Galatians 3:26–29, NRSV).

SERMON

It's Time[2]

There was a sharp dispute. The church called for a meeting and delegates travelled long distances to get there. When they arrived, there was disagreement. It got nasty at times. There was a debate.

I'm not talking about General Synod 2016, which took place this past week. I'm talking about our reading from the 15th chapter of Acts, the account of the Jerusalem Council of 50 A.D., the first recorded general synod of our church almost 2,000 years ago. The matter being debated was of critical importance: could non-Jews become members of the church, and, if so, did they need to be circumcised in accordance with the Jewish law?

Apostles such as Peter, Paul, and Barnabas had been doing the very thing that Jesus had called them to do, proclaiming the gospel to the ends of the earth and to all nations. Not only Jews, but Greeks and other Gentile peoples were responding to that call, proclaiming Jesus as Lord, being baptized and filled with the power of the Holy Spirit. Seeing this, many in the church were calling for Gentile believers to be circumcised, just as God through Moses had commanded all Jews to be circumcised as a sign of God's covenant with his people.

Those calling for circumcision had tradition on their side. Those calling for circumcision could quote the scriptures to make their case.

But some people, apostles such as Peter, Paul, and Barnabas, perceived that God was doing something new. They discerned a new and powerful movement of the Spirit of God. And they shared what they had seen with the gathered assembly, telling them what God was doing amongst the Gentiles based on their own first-hand encounters and experience.

When the debate began, the traditionalists stood up and insisted that "the Gentiles must be circumcised and be required to keep the law of Moses." They did so in good faith. After all, that was their understanding of what was required to be part of God's people.

But Peter, the one who had received a great vision of inclusion, the one whom God had told to go and meet Cornelius, the Roman centurion, Peter got up and addressed the assembly: "God, who knows the heart, showed that he accepted the Gentiles by giving the Holy Spirit to them, just as he did to us."

And that great synod in Jerusalem in 50 A.D. had a change of heart. By doing away with the need for circumcision, it opened the doors to the full inclusion of Gentiles in the church.

Not everyone agreed with the synod's decision. In the years that followed, there continued to be those who called for circumcision, those that wanted Gentile believers to look and behave like Jews. And so, likely a few years after the council, Paul wrote his letter to the Galatians. He wanted to ground the decision of the Jerusalem Council in a new theological understanding, a new way of understanding what it means to be the people of God, the children of God. He rooted this new understanding in baptism.

Paul wrote, "for in Christ Jesus you are all children of God through faith. As many of you as were baptized into Christ have clothed yourselves with Christ. There is no longer Jew or Greek, there is no longer slave or free, there is no longer male and female; for all of you are one in Christ Jesus."

The Spirit of God moved in the early church in the first century, and Gentiles were fully welcomed into the church as children of God, through baptism into Christ. Without this movement of the Spirit that took place in the first century, none of us would be here in this church today. But we are here. We who are baptized are all children of God; there is no longer Jew or Gentile. This is our church.

In the 18th and 19th centuries, there was another movement of the Spirit. The Spirit of God spoke powerfully through people like William Wilberforce, Hannah More, and others against the injustice and inhumanity of the slave trade. And though they faced great opposition in society, and though the church was divided, eventually they prevailed and the slave trade in the British Empire was abolished. "Amazing grace," wrote the former slave ship captain John Newton, who sorrowfully repented his involvement in slavery. "I once was lost but now am found, was blind but now I see." All who are baptized are one in Christ. There is no longer Jew or Gentile, neither slave nor free.

In the 20th century, the Spirit of God moved again. For most of our church history, almost 2,000 years, women have been excluded from positions of leadership in the church. Again, there were theological arguments. Again, there were scriptural passages that supported the tradition. But again, the Holy Spirit moved. In our Anglican Church of Canada, there was another bruising debate, there was conflict, there were deep differences. But we decided in our General Synod of 1973 to proceed with the ordination of women. In 1976, six pioneering and perseverant women – Patricia Reed, Mary Mills, Elspeth Alley, Virginia Briant, Mary Lucas, and Beverly Shanley – were the first women ordained as priests in the Anglican Church of Canada. Over the past 40 years, we as a church have been blessed by the ministry and leadership of many women, ordained and lay, and the fruit of the Spirit has been abundantly clear for us to see. All who are baptized are one in Christ. There is neither Jew nor Gentile, slave nor free, no longer male and female.

My friends, it is the 21st century and I believe that the Spirit of God is once more moving powerfully in our midst. Now, I could be wrong. None of us has a monopoly on discerning the movement of God's Spirit. That's why we do our discernment in community, by sharing our experiences, by meditating on the word of God, by praying together. That is what we did last week, over 200 of us, at the General Synod of the Anglican Church of Canada, not for the first time, but as part of a process and discernment that has been going on for the last 40 years. This discernment will continue. We have not acted hastily; many would say that we have acted much too slowly.

At our General Synod, after much conversation and much debate, we voted to change the marriage canon of the Anglican Church of Canada to provide for same-sex marriage. We reaffirmed the integrity and sanctity of committed adult same-sex relationships. Lesbian, gay, bisexual, transgender, and queer people are to be fully included in the life, leadership, and sacraments of the church, including marriage. Though it will take three years and another vote to realize this change in church legislation, in our diocese of Ottawa, Bishop Chapman has made this change effective immediately as a pastoral measure.

So to those of you who are lesbian, gay, bisexual, transgender, or queer, may I say simply this and be able to fully mean it for the first time: Welcome. This is your church.

And may I also say this. It has been your faithful witness within our church that has provided the impetus for this change. Over and over again at General Synod, we spoke about the faith, the godliness, the beauty, and the holiness of your lives, your relationships, and your witness and service within the church and in the world. Just as Peter said of the Gentiles that God, who knows everyone's heart, showed that they were accepted by giving the Holy Spirit to them just as the Spirit was given to us, we say the same thing about so many of you in the church. You have endured many years of exclusion and hostility, and all the pain that goes with that, and yet you are shining examples of the love of God at work in God's children. Thank you, and I'm sorry that it took so long.

There are in our midst, across the country, and sitting right here with us, people who in good faith disagree with the decision made by General Synod. There are many who in good faith have a well-thought-out and prayerful understanding of scripture and theology that compels them to disagree with same-sex marriage. I know this to be true, for that was once how I thought. To you I want to say that you are welcome here. It is good that you are here. We welcome and celebrate diversity in our church, including theological diversity. As we will sing together in a few minutes, "we need each other more than we need to agree."

I know first-hand from our recent experience at General Synod how disagreements can be hurtful and how bonds of friendship can be strained. Some people – a small minority but too many – said hurtful things. Please pray for each other and for the unity of our church. Be gentle with each other. Remember the commandment Jesus gave to us on the night of his death: "Love each other as I have loved you." To those in our midst who are troubled or who disagree with the results of our General Synod, I want to say thank you for being with us today and for having the grace to allow those of us who need to celebrate the outcome of General Synod to do so.

Every morning at General Synod, we began our day with prayer and with a reading from the book of the prophet Isaiah: "This is what the Lord says... Forget the former things; do not dwell on the past. See I am doing a new thing! Now it springs up; do you not perceive it?"

This is a historic moment for our church. The Lord is indeed doing a new thing.

1. The complete text of *This Holy Estate* can be found here: http://www.anglican.ca/wp-content/uploads/ Marriage_Canon_REPORT_15Sept22.pdf (accessed March 4, 2017).
2. Sermon: July 17, 2016. On the occasion of the General Synod resolution to change the marriage canon to provide for same-sex marriage. Readings: Acts 15:1– 12; Psalm 118:1–2, 14–24, Galatians 3:21–28; John 15:12– 17.

SIXTEEN

The Better Story

The days shorten. The air becomes crisp and cold and the first snowflakes fall from the sky onto frozen earth below. The closing of each calendar year gives us the opportunity to look back, to reflect on the stories we have heard, and on the stories we have told over the past 12 months. The stories that lift us up and the stories that drag us down. We enter the season of Advent and anticipate once more the Christmas holidays, dreading the frantic activity that they so often bring, but hoping for the calm of a few days removed from our normal routines, to be with family and friends for those of us so blessed to have them. We have our Christmas traditions. For many of us, the most meaningful of these is to leave the warmth of home and to travel through the darkness of the night and into the church on Christmas Eve, where we will hear our story once more.

And it came to pass in those days, that there went out a decree from Caesar Augustus that all the world should be taxed. (And this taxing was first made when Cyrenius was governor of Syria.) And all went to be taxed, every one into his own city. And Joseph also went up from Galilee, out of the city of Nazareth, into Judaea, unto the city of David, which is called Bethlehem; (because he was of the house and lineage of David), to be taxed with Mary his espoused wife, being great with child.

And so it was, that, while they were there, the days were

accomplished that she should be delivered. And she brought forth her firstborn son, and wrapped him in swaddling clothes, and laid him in a manger; because there was no room for them in the inn.

And there were in the same country shepherds abiding in the field, keeping watch over their flock by night. And, lo, the angel of the Lord came upon them, and the glory of the Lord shone round about them: and they were sore afraid. And the angel said unto them,

"Fear not: for, behold, I bring you good tidings of great joy, which shall be to all people. For unto you is born this day in the city of David a Saviour, which is Christ the Lord. And this shall be a sign unto you; Ye shall find the babe wrapped in swaddling clothes, lying in a manger."

And suddenly there was with the angel a multitude of the heavenly host praising God, and saying, "Glory to God in the highest, and on earth peace, good will toward men" (Luke 2:1–14, *KJV*).

SERMON

The Better Story[1]

As I was doing laundry a few days ago, I walked past the **TV** with a basket of wet clothes in my hands. On TV was *A Charlie Brown Christmas*, and it was just at the part where Charlie Brown throws back his head and cries out, "Isn't there anyone who knows what Christmas is all about?" Linus says, "Sure Charlie Brown, I can tell you what Christmas is all about," and he walks out onto the stage and recites the story from the Gospel of Luke, which we just heard. Even though I've heard the story a thousand times, and even though I was in a hurry to get on with all the things I had to do, I stopped, stood still, and listened to the story, the basket of wet laundry heavy in my hands.

Why do we want to listen to this story?

Maybe it's because there's something about it that's different from most of the stories we hear. Think about this past year. What were the stories that we heard most often, the stories that were in the news, the stories that had the biggest impact on us as individuals and as a society?

There was the story of the Syrian refugee crisis, of the ongoing civil war in Syria and of the millions of refugees trying to get to Europe; of the barbed wire fences erected to keep them out and of the death by drowning of a young boy who washed up on a Turkish beach.

There was terrorism. The heinous acts of the Islamic State in Iraq and Syria and beyond. The attacks in Paris. The response to those attacks: increased bombing and Donald Trump calling for a ban on all Muslims entering the United States. The questions about what comes next...

There was our own election here in Canada, told mostly as a story of who's winning and who's losing, complete with daily polls, attack ads, negative campaigning, and plenty of nastiness on social media. Election promises to ban *niqabs* and a "snitch" line for barbaric cultural practices.

There was the report of the Truth and Reconciliation Commission that revealed in intimate detail the cultural genocide of our Indigenous peoples perpetrated over the course of more than a century, instigated by our government and aided by our church.

These are just *some* of the stories that we told ourselves over the past year. Stories of insecurity. Stories of conflict and division. Stories of winners and losers. Stories of power and oppression. Stories of anxiety and fear.

And there's a problem here, though it's not that these stories shouldn't be told. The problem is that when we're immersed in stories like these, when they become the air that we breathe, when we see ourselves as actors, or perhaps as helpless bystanders in these stories, what happens? What does it do to us?

These stories diminish us. They bring us down. They make us less than what we *could* be. They alienate us from each other. They make us afraid.

But we have a *better* story. A story of hope. A story of new life. A story of promise. A story that says, "Do not be afraid."

We heard that story again this evening.

Now, the way Luke tells it, at first you might think that this story is no different than the others. It seems to begin in the same old way: "And it came to pass in those days, that there went out a decree from Caesar Augustus, that all the world should be taxed."

Here we go again. Another story about how the powerful dictate our lives. Caesar Augustus, maybe the most powerful man in all of history, issuing a decree. We know how Rome operates. Power. Decrees. Migrants forced to travel.

But then, as quickly as he appeared, the Emperor Augustus disappears, drops out of the story. And the focus shifts instead to an unlikely couple in an awkward situation.

"And Joseph also went up from Galilee, out of the city of Nazareth into Judea, unto the city of David which is called Bethlehem... He went to be registered with Mary, to whom he was engaged and who was expecting a child."

It is an awkward situation, Joseph with his pregnant fiancée, forced to travel at the worst possible time. But we're given just a hint of promise. There's an air of expectancy as they arrive in Bethlehem, the city of David.

"While they were there, the time came for her to deliver her child. And she gave birth to her firstborn son and wrapped him in bands of cloth and laid him in a manger, because there was no room for them in the inn."

The birth of a child. Completely ordinary, yet always extraordinary. You know the feeling. But why this child, why has this child suddenly become the focus of our story? What does this birth mean?

Or as Charlie Brown would say, "Isn't there anyone who knows what Christmas is all about?"

And here the story twists again in an unexpected direction, as the people who are about to discover the meaning of the baby's birth are probably the most unlikely candidates you could imagine: poor, uneducated, homeless, shunned by polite society. There were in that region, "shepherds, abiding in the fields, keeping watch over their flocks by night.

"And lo, an angel of the Lord came upon them, and the glory of the Lord shone round about them, and they were terrified.

"But the angel said to them, 'Be not afraid, for see, I bring you good news of great joy for all the people. For unto you is born this day in the city of David a Saviour who is Christ the Lord.'"

A saviour? Do we need to be saved? It's a word that's often misunderstood. Sometimes people are told that being saved is about escaping judgment and going to heaven after we die. But that's not what Luke means. The word he uses for salvation can also be translated as to be healed or to be made whole. The salvation that the angels proclaim is about being restored to wholeness. It's about being rescued from alienation in our relationships with each other and with God. And it's about knowing that God is with us and that we no longer have to be afraid.

This is good news of great joy and it's for *all* people. Even for shepherds. Even for unwed teenage mothers. Even for you and for me. No wonder that "all who heard it were amazed at what the shepherds told them."

This is the story that we tell this evening.

What happens when we immerse ourselves in this story, rather than all the other stories that surround us? What would that do to us?

This is a story that has the power to lift us up. A story that encourages us to live fully, to live into the fullness of who we were created to be. A story that can lift the weight of fear and anxiety from our shoulders, and give us the courage to reach out across divisions even in the midst of conflict. This is a story that can inspire us to be peacemakers, to be agents of reconciliation, to be instruments of compassion, and to love others, because this is the story of a God who came to be with us, as one of us, out of great love, not in the comfort of an emperor's palace but rather in a manger, in a little village, surrounded by shepherds, because there was no room at the inn.

So tonight we immerse ourselves in this story. We marvel at the glow of the light that shines in the darkness. We sing the carols, sing the songs that proclaim the story over and over again.

Share peace, come to the table, warm to the company of those around you. Open yourselves to awe and wonder, if only for this night. For we have been given the better story that, even in the midst of darkness, there is a light that shines in our world; even in the midst of fear, there is a love that will prevail. The people who walk in darkness have seen a great light; for unto us a child is born, unto us a son is given, and he shall be called Immanuel, God with us, the Prince of Peace.

1. Sermon: Christmas Eve 2015. Readings: Isaiah 9:2–7;
    Psalm 96; Titus 2:11–14; Luke 2:1–20.

MARK WHITTALL

The Rev. Mark Whittall is the pastor of St. Albans Church and a priest of the Anglican Diocese of Ottawa. He is an engineer by training, and obtained graduate degrees in Theoretical Physics and in Development Economics from Oxford University. His first career was as an engineer and executive in the high-tech sector, rising to the position of CEO and earning recognition as Ottawa's Entrepreneur of the Year in 2000. Soon afterwards he left his business career and turned to the study of theology. He served as Professor, History of Science at Augustine College in Ottawa from 2002 to 2007 and was ordained as an Anglican Priest in 2008. After a brief stay in a rural parish, he was tasked with building a new congregation at St. Albans Church in downtown Ottawa in 2011, where he currently serves as pastor.

From the St. Albans website

Mark became the Incumbent of St. Albans Church in 2011. Mark was born in Montreal and grew up in Manotick, Ontario near Ottawa. His studies took him to Queen's in Kingston and Oxford in the UK, where he completed degrees in engineering, physics and development economics.

He returned to Ottawa to begin his career in technology and international development in 1987. His work with Intelcan took him around the world. In 2005 he returned to university, this time to St. Paul University in Ottawa where he completed his Masters in Pastoral Theology in 2008. Mark was ordained as a priest of the Anglican Diocese of Ottawa in 2008 and served as Incumbent of the Parish of Huntley in Carp until 2011.

The move to St. Albans in downtown Ottawa provided the opportunity to build a new congregation and to learn how to do and be church in new and exciting ways. Mark tells the story of St. Albans re-birth in his 2016 book ReInvention: Stories from an Urban Church. Ministry at St. Albans provides Mark with a unique opportunity to engage with diverse groups of people of all ages and backgrounds, including the folks at Centre 454 and students at the University of Ottawa. Mark also has a passion for working with children, a passion which is evident in his puppet collection!

At home, Mark shares his life with Guylaine, his wife of 26 years, and his two children, Jonathan, 23 and Michelle, 21. In his leisure time he enjoys sports, music and even a bit of quantum physics. His most recent book is ReImagine: Preaching in the Present Tense, which is about what happens when we let the stories of our lives intersect the stories of our faith.

From Bloomberg.com

Mr. Mark Whittall was the Founder and served as Chairman and Chief Executive Officer of Sybridge Technologies, Inc. Mr. Whittall served as Chief Executive Officer of Intelcan Technosystems Inc. since 1998 and also served as its President, a global provider of Air Traffic Management and Wireless Telecom Solutions, which was recognized as one of Canada's fastest growing high technology companies by the *Financial Post* magazine. He served as Chairman and Director of Intelcan Technosystems Inc. Mr. Whittall is a Professional Engineer. He holds an engineering degree from Queen's University and Masters degrees in both Physics and Economics from Oxford University.

WOOD LAKE

Imagining, living, and telling the faith story.

WOOD LAKE IS THE FAITH STORY COMPANY.

It has told
- the story of the seasons of the earth, the people of God, and the place and purpose of faith in the world;
- the story of the faith journey, from birth to death;
- the story of Jesus and the churches that carry his message.

Wood Lake has been telling stories for more than 35 years. During that time, it has given form and substance to the words, songs, pictures, and ideas of hundreds of storytellers.

Those stories have taken a multitude of forms – parables, poems, drawings, prayers, epiphanies, songs, books, paintings, hymns, curricula – all driven by a common mission of serving those on the faith journey.

Wood Lake Publishing Inc.
485 Beaver Lake Road
Kelowna, BC, Canada V4V 1S5
250.766.2778

www.woodlake.com